· HAIL CAESAR ·

Written By:

Rick Priestley

Cover Artwork:

Peter Dennis

Photography:

Alan Perry, Michael Perry,
Kevin Dallimore,
Duncan Macfarlane, Eric Hagen
and Wargames Illustrated

Design and Layout:

Paul Sawyer and Tim Vincent

Editing:

Duncan Macfarlane and Mark Owen

With Special Thanks To:

Bennett Blalock-Doane, Dr Phil Hendry,
The Phoenix Wargames Club,
Paul Tysoe, Carl King, The Worcester
Wargames Club, Andy Bartlett,
Pete Brown, James Manto, Neil Smith,
Craig Woodfield and Scott K.

ISBN: 978-0-9563581-3-4

© Copyright Warlord Games Ltd. 2011

www.warlordgames.com

D1492973

Opposing hoplites engaged in battle

CONTENTS

A Roman mile fort prepares to resist rampaging raiders

CARRY ON CAESAR!

This supplement to Warlord Games' Hail Caesar rulebook contains army lists and gaming stats for no fewer than sixty three armies of the ancient world. The armies included in this book take us from the dawn of civilisation up to the mid-third century AD. A second supplement will cover the armies of late antiquity up to the early middle ages.

Our army lists include stats for all of the best-known and widely collected forces for which 28mm sized models are currently available. Of course it is impossible to provide stats for every nation or culture that bore arms over the several thousand years covered. Those seeking further examples, or details for more obscure or exotic armies are therefore referred to: www.warlordgames.com.

Of the many people who have helped put these lists together I would particularly like to thank Dr Phil Hendry and Paul Tysoe for their very timely and informed contributions. I'd also like to thank all those who have commented and provided ideas via the various on-line forums.

OBJECTIVE OF THE LISTS

The Hail Caesar rulebook provides standardised or typical stat values for different kinds of troops, and these can be used to represent any ancient or early medieval army. The rulebook also includes a selection of special rules that we have found useful for tailoring armies to our own requirements. We imagine other players will wish to devise their own special rules and create armies in the same fashion as ourselves – based on their own reading of history, fiction, film, TV or upon their imagination. In this respect a book of army lists such as this is not strictly required to play Hail Caesar.

During the early development of the rules it was assumed that players wouldn't be much interested in army lists. However, as the game developed more players became involved in our battles, and they began to ask about stats and special rules for armies they already owned. I therefore decided to put this volume together to demonstrate how the most popular armies can be represented using the Hail Caesar rule system.

The purpose of these lists is therefore to provide examples of the kind of stats and special rules that we would typically use to represent the armies described. In addition the lists contain army composition guidelines that define the proportions of different troops available to a typical force. Lastly the lists give points values for different units, so that players who feel the need can arrange to play games with armies selected to a predetermined points total.

REFERENCES AND NOTES

The header for each army list gives its title and the era covered by the list, for example, *Sassanid Persian 3rd – 6th Century AD*. The lists are presented broadly in chronological order, although with some armies covering longer time periods than others there is inevitably a fair amount of overlap. Immediately below the title I have listed a series of key *search* words that describe leaders, battles or campaigns associated with that particular army. If you enter any of these into your internet search engine you will find information about the history and background of the chosen army. I have tried to select words and phrases that are most readily recognised by search engines, which is why some of the spellings or names may be variants of the army's title or other words used in the lists.

I have included a short historical gloss, but on the whole I have avoided writing a potted history of each army as that would have taken up a great deal of space that could otherwise be used to present more armies. For historical background I refer readers to the key search words as explained above. The introduction to each army also includes any additional special rules or variants of rules, but I have only added these where I thought they were pretty much essential to the character of the army. The main purpose of these notes is to explain the choices I made when it came to representing the different troop types, and in some cases to provide alternatives or to point out where a specific historical context might inform an army's composition.

GAMING VALUES

Stats for the different types of troops are given in the format shown below. As you can see this is the same format as used in Hail Caesar with the addition of a column for the points value. By-and-large these conform to the values given in the Troop Types section of Hail Caesar and should therefore come as no surprise.

Unit		Combat			Morale Save	Stamina	Special	Points Value
	Clash	Sustained	Short Range	Long Range				
Heavy infantry elite hoplites armed with long spears	7	7	3/0	0	4+	6	Phalanx, Elite	35 per unit

TROOP VALUES

Hittites and allies pouring from behind the walls of Kadesh.

Unit: The name of the unit (hoplites, legionaries, spearmen, etc), the basic type (heavy infantry, medium infantry, etc) and weapons carried (spears, javelins and swords, long spears, etc).

Combat: The four combat values each indicate the number of attack dice rolled in hand-to-hand or ranged fighting: Clash, Sustained, Short Range, and Long Range.

Clash: The number of attacks in the first round of each and every hand-to-hand combat.

Sustained: The number of attacks in all subsequent rounds of hand-to-hand combat.

Short Range: This is both the number of attacks used when supporting in hand-to-hand combat, and the number of attacks for ranged shooting and skirmishing up to 6" distance. If a single value is shown it is used for both. If two values are shown the first is used for supporting and the second is used for ranged attacks. Split values such as these are commonly used for troops that carry no missile weapons and which are unable to make short ranged attacks although they can still support, e.g. pikemen.

Long Range: The number of attacks made over 6" distance

and up to the maximum range of the weapon carried. Typically such troops carry bows, slings or crossbows.

Morale Save: The minimum dice score required to negate a successful enemy attack – i.e. the unit's 'save'. The save is related to the amount of armour worn and the size of shields carried, because these things offer both physical and psychological protection. Troops usually wear armour because they expect to get stuck in and fight at close quarters, but some troops are quite happy to plunge into combat while practically – or even literally – naked.

Stamina: The number of casualties a unit can take before it is 'shaken' with all that entails. The stamina value is the maximum number of casualties that can be recorded onto a unit from turn-to-turn, and it is usually 6 for standard sized units, 4 for small units, 8 for large units and 3 for artillery.

Special: This column indicates any 'useful rules' that are applied as well as referencing any rules specific to that list. See the appendix for more about these.

Points Value: The points value of the unit or, in some cases, the extra points paid for a unit upgrade or a reduction applied either to reduce the unit's size or to give it a disadvantageous special rule.

COMPOSITION GUIDELINES

The composition guidelines are intended to reflect the historical strengths and weaknesses of the armies concerned. There is no need to stick rigidly to these if players prefer not to. A scenario may call for a specific mix of troops, in which case the guidelines may not be appropriate.

The guidelines define the proportion of infantry to cavalry and other types as indicated at the start of each list. This is given in the format shown below. This example is from the Imperial Roman list.

Infantry 50%+ — At least half the units in the army must be infantry other than skirmishers.

Legions 25%+ of infantry — At least a quarter of the non-skirmisher infantry units in the army must be legionaries of one type or another.

Cavalry up to 25% — Up to a quarter of the units in the army can be cavalry.

Artillery — There must be at least three legionary units for every artillery unit fielded, and no more heavy or medium artillery than light artillery units in total.

Divisions 4 units+ — Divisions must contain at least 4 units excluding skirmishers and must be led by a commander.

Skirmishers per division 50% of infantry — Divisions can contain up to half as many skirmisher units as they contain non-skirmisher infantry.

The number of divisions in the army is not fixed, although in most cases a division must contain at least four units not counting skirmishers. Aside from this obligation, the player is free to organise his army into as many divisions as he wishes. Division commanders are generally free but occasionally incur a cost as noted in the list itself. One division commander must be nominated as the general in the usual way.

As a general principle I have separated out skirmishers and limited the number that can be included in mixed divisions. I have done this to place some limits on their ability to act independently, and hence their overall effectiveness compared to battle line troops. For example, in the example given above a division could contain four units of Roman legionaries plus up to two units of skirmishers (i.e. half the number of non-skirmisher infantry).

In addition some units can only be fielded in limited numbers, often just one, whilst others can be upgraded within certain limits as in the examples below. These examples also come from the Imperial Roman list.

TROOP VALUES

Unit	Clash	Sustained	Short Range	Long Range	Morale Save	Stamina	Special	Points Value
Heavy infantry legionaries armed with pila and swords	7	7	3	0	4+	6	Drilled, Testudo	32 per unit
• Extra to upgrade legionaries to elite – up to half	7	7	3	0	4+	6	Drilled, Elite, Testudo	+3 per unit
• Extra to upgrade legionaries to veteran – up to 1 unit	7	7	3	0	4+	6	Drilled, Elite, Tough fighters, Stubborn, Testudo	+7 per unit

The limitations on the proportions of different troop types, and the restrictions on the numbers of some specific units, mean that armies chosen using these guidelines will present a mix of troops that is historically credible and tolerably playable within the context of our game.

POINTS VALUES

I have worked out points values for each unit to reflect its broad capabilities within the game. The greater the points value, the better the unit is in most situations. Of course, circumstances may sometimes dictate that troops perform better or worse than one might expect, either because of unfavourable terrain or some combination of opposing troops. We must learn to be sanguine about such things.

My intention here is simply to allow players to arrange games between comparably sized forces where they wish to do so, for example at a club meeting where each of four players might agree to bring along 300 points to contribute towards a combined force.

The calculation for working out points values is given separately and at length in the appendix, should players wish to work out values for further troop types or new armies.

SIZE OF ARMIES

The lists are primarily designed for choosing armies of between three and six divisions, with something like four to six units in each division. A small force would therefore comprise twelve units in three divisions. Restrictions placed on the availability of some units assume armies within these limits. If players wish to field especially large armies they might wish to adjust these minimums proportionately, and we leave this up to players to decide for themselves.

A satisfactory game can be played in a few hours with 300 points per side. This is sufficient to field three divisions in most armies. Double this value, 600 points, gives a game that can still be concluded in an evening quite easily. Obviously, with larger armies it is advantageous to have several players on each side as described in the Hail Caesar rulebook.

MAKING USE OF THESE LISTS

The Hail Caesar rules have been developed to play the kind of games its author and contributors enjoy: namely, multi-player scenario-based battles with an umpire who not only moderates play, but usually determines victory conditions and concocts any special rules that are needed. We found it soon became necessary to write down the stats for the various troops, if only to save the effort of re-inventing them for every game! As we played more games we experimented with different ways of representing different troops, sometimes entirely successfully and sometimes less so. Eventually, we honed our sense of judgement, and after a while we came to accept that some types of troops were best fielded as small units, or with standard useful rules, or with specific combinations of fighting values. The lists in this supplement demonstrate these principles. For example, light cavalry and horse archers are almost always fielded as small units because this puts them into a skirmishing and supporting role as seems generally most appropriate.

The stats given, and the application of useful rules, demonstrate our approach. They are not meant to be definitive or binding. They are examples. If players intend to portray particular armies as they appeared at specific battles then they will no doubt wish to use their specialist knowledge to determine the opposing forces. One obvious example of such variation is to make units elite, or raw, or levy as seems most credible – because troops could begin a campaign as one and easily end it as another! The interpretations provided by the lists are inevitably generalised to some extent. In our own battles we would quite happily adjust a stat slightly, or add or even invent a useful rule for a game if that suited our purpose. We would suggest that umpires creating scenarios and running games look upon our lists as a helpful starting point and nothing more.

The composition guidelines are intended to reflect the character and general appearance of the actual armies described, as far as this is possible to gauge when dealing with battles fought so many hundreds of years ago. We would not think to apply these proportions strictly in our own scenario-based games, leaving the composition of the armies up to whoever has devised the scenario instead. However, it is worth pointing out that our collections have been built to represent their historic prototypes and so tend to fall within the parameters given. These proportions are intended to give players an 'at a glance' idea of what a typical army looks like. For example, is it mostly infantry with a few cavalry, a good mix of both, or an army that is predominantly made up of horsemen? Although this will undoubtedly be useful for players new to the world of 'ancients', there can be very few old hands with expert knowledge of **all** the armies represented. I therefore hope that the guidelines will prove useful to all players whether they choose to make full use of them or not.

Finally we come to the points values. These have been included so that players can choose armies to a predetermined value, as many readers who already own ancient armies, and fight ancient battles, will be used to that kind of format. Hail Caesar is different from most sets of rules in that it is not designed for fighting matched armies in strict competition. It is primarily aimed at playing umpired scenarios in the fashion depicted in the rulebook. However, there is no denying it is often convenient to be able to talk in terms of a 300, 400 or whatever points army, especially when arranging to play games at clubs, get-togethers or against new opponents. The formula used to calculate the points value is given separately in the appendix, together with some further discussion of how it is applied.

A NOTE ON USEFUL RULES

I have included more about the various useful rules and how they are applied in the appendix (see page 80). At this stage it is worth saying that I have selected from all the useful rules only those I felt were applicable in a general context without either slowing down play or introducing too much unpredictability. I have adopted a 'light touch', as my feeling is that this keeps the basic framework of the game solid, and is sufficient to characterise the units concerned. Those who favour a more generous approach (and whose memories are up to the task!) can easily apply or devise more useful rules as they wish and they are welcome to do so.

A FINAL NOTE ON CHRONOLOGY

The armies are listed roughly in order of earliest first, though as some armies cover longer time spans than others there is necessarily some overlap. I have given only approximate dates for the armies described, and where a specific date may be relevant I have usually mentioned this in the notes. Bear in mind I have used the traditional chronology when fixing dates for the Late Bronze Age, as opposed to the New Chronology championed by David Rohl amongst others. This is because the mass of current research uses the traditional dating, and to try and reconcile the two is simply too great a task to attempt for a set of army lists. However, where the New Chronology suggests potential synchronicity I have tended to point this out as a matter of general interest.

This is the Egyptian army of the Old and Middle Kingdom prior to the introduction of the chariot. As such it is often neglected in favour of the army of the New Kingdom with its chariots and more exotic troop types. None the less it is an interesting combination of native and allied troops and a good match for its historic opponents.

Search: The Pyramid Age, The First Intermediate Period, The Hyksos and the Second Intermediary Period.

Archers 25%+	At least a quarter of the non-skirmisher units in the army must be medium infantry archers including any Ahauty archers.
Ahauty up to 25%	Up to a quarter of the non-skirmisher units in the army can be Ahauty (hereditary warriors).
Divisions 4+ units	Divisions must contain at least 4 units excluding skirmishers and must be led by a commander.
Skirmishers per division 50% of infantry	Divisions may contain up to a half as many skirmisher units as they contain non-skirmisher infantry.

Old & Middle Kingdom Egyptian Troop Values

Unit	Combat				Morale Save	Stamina	Special	Points Value
	Clash	Sustained	Short Range	Long Range				
Henu Nefru Egyptian medium infantry with stabbing spears and shields	6	6	3/0	0	5+	6	Levy	20 per unit
• *Extra to make Henu Nefru mercenary Nubians – up to half such units*	6	6	3/0	0	5+	6		*+3 per unit*
Ahauty Egyptian medium infantry with stabbing spears and shields	6	6	3/0	0	5+	6		23 per unit
Ahauty Egyptian medium infantry with eye-axes and shields	7	6	2/0	0	5+	6		23 per unit
Shemsu Egyptian medium infantry with double-handed axes – up to 1 unit per division	7	6	2/0	0	5+	6	Tough fighters	25 per unit
Egyptian medium infantry militia archers	5	5	3	3	5+	6	Levy	21 per unit
• *Extra to make archers mercenary Nubians – up to half such units*	5	5	3	3	5+	6		*+ 3 per unit*
Ahauty Egyptian medium infantry archers	5	5	3	3	5+	6		24 per unit
Libyan or Kushite light infantry archers fielded as small units	3	3	2	2	0	4		14 per unit
Skirmishers with javelins fielded as small units	3	2	2	0	0	4	Levy	9 per unit
• *Extra to give skirmishers slings as Semite nomads – up to 1 unit*	2	2	2	2	0	4	Levy	*+1 per unit*
• *Extra to give skirmishers bows as Semite or Nubians – up to 1 unit*	2	2	2	2	0	4	Levy	*+1 per unit*
Commanders	1 commander must be provided per division. All commanders including general have leadership 8.							Free

Chariots clash at the Battle of Kadesh.

NUBIAN

Kush lies to the south of Egypt and is known as Nubia in later times. Its people are primitive, barbarous and exceptionally fierce – so much so that they are often recruited as mercenaries by the Egyptian pharoahs.

Search: Medjay, The Kingdom of Kerma, The Kingdom of Kush.

Skirmishing archers 25%+	At least a quarter of units in the army must be skirmishers with bows.
Divisions 4+ units	Divisions must contain at least 4 units and must be led by a commander. Guard must form part of the general's division.
Skirmishers per division 100% of infantry or all	Divisions may contain as many skirmisher units as they contain non-skirmisher infantry, or alternatively they may contain all skirmishers.

Nubian Troop Values

Unit	Clash	Sustained	Short Range	Long Range	Morale Save	Stamina	Special	Points Value
Nubian Guard – light infantry with bows and javelins	5	5	3	3	6+	6	Eager, Marksmen, Valiant	27 per unit
Nubian light infantry with mixed javelins and bows	5	5	3	1	6+	6	Eager	21 per unit
Nubian light infantry warband with mixed javelins and bows	7	5	2	1	6+	6	Eager	22 per unit
• *Make warband wild fighters*	7	5	2	1	6+	6	*Eager, Wild fighters*	*+3 per unit*
• *Make warband frenzied – up to 1 unit*	7	5	2	1	6+	6	*Frenzied charge, Eager, Wild fighters*	*+6 per unit*
Skirmishers with javelins	5	4	3	0	0	6	Eager	18 per unit
Skirmishers with bows	4	4	3	3	0	6	Eager	20 per unit
Commanders	1 commander must be provided per division. The general has leadership 8. All other commanders have leadership 7							Free

AKKAD AND SUMER

These are the armies of the world's earliest empires. In these distant times Mesopotamia was divided into small city states that were constantly at war with each other. The very first chariots appear during this period and are drawn by wild asses – called onagers. Proper horse-drawn chariots make an appearance about 2000 BC. Onager chariots are drawn by four wild asses – we shall treat them as light chariots with a span of four and suggest basing them as heavy chariots. Because of their ferocious ill temper and the legendary intractability of the wild ass, any order given to an onager chariot unit or division of which it is a part will blunder on a roll of 11 or 12.

Search: Eannatum of Lagash, Stele of the Vultures, Ur-Nammu, Akkadian Empire, Sargon the Great.

Chariots up to 25%	Up to a quarter of the units in the army can comprise chariots.
Infantry 75%+	At least three quarters of the units in the army must comprise infantry other than skirmishers.
Sumerian or Akkadian spearmen or Royal Guard 25%+ of infantry	At least a quarter of the non-skirmisher infantry units must be either Sumerian/Akkadian medium infantry with long spears, or Royal Guard.
Divisions 4+ units	Divisions must contain at least 4 units excluding skirmishers and must be led by a commander.
Skirmishers per division 50% of infantry	Divisions may contain up to half as many skirmisher units as they contain non-skirmisher infantry.

Akkad & Sumer Troop Values

Unit	Clash	Sustained	Short Range	Long Range	Morale Save	Stamina	Special	Points Value
Sumerian or Akkadian medium infantry with long spears	6	6	3/0	0	5+	6		23 per unit
Royal Guard medium infantry with double-handed weapons and throw-sticks – 1 unit maximum	7	6	2	0	5+	6	Tough fighters	25 per unit
Sumerian or Akkadian light infantry archers	4	4	3	3	0	6		20 per unit
Skirmishers with javelins fielded as small units	3	2	2	0	0	4		11 per unit
Skirmishers with slings fielded as small units	2	2	2	2	0	4	Levy	10 per unit
Amorite skirmishers with bows fielded as small units – up to 1 per Amorite warband	2	2	2	2	0	4		12 per unit
Amorite medium infantry tribal warband with spears, javelins and bows	7	6	2	0	6+	6	Wild fighters	25 per unit
Gutian light infantry with double-handed weapons and throw sticks fielded as small units	5	4	1	0	6+	4	Marauders	18 per unit
Elamite light infantry archers fielded as small units	4	4	2	2	0	4	Marauders	18 per unit
Onager-drawn light chariots with javelin-armed crews	6	6	3	0	4+	6	See notes	27 per unit
Commanders		1 commander must be provided per division. All commanders including general have leadership 8.						Free

AMORITE BABYLONIA

20th–16th centuries BC

This is the army of Babylon under Hammurabi which drove the Elamites back from Mesopotamia and established an empire that stretched from Mari to Ur. Chariots are now a firmly established part of armies of the Near East. The option to field Sabum Kabitum as spearmen reflects earlier Akkadian tactical practice and allows us to field an army from before the rise of the Amorite dynasty of Babylon (c.1894 BC). Sabum Kabitum means 'heavily armed' and describes the regular, trained troops who had something by way of armour. Sabum Quallatum means 'lightly armed'. By Hammurabi's day Babylonian troops fought with shorter spears and javelins in the Amorite style. This list can also be used for the succeeding Kassite period that emerged after the sack of Babylon by the Hittites (c.1585 BC). It will also serve to represent any of the Amorite Kingdoms of which Babylon was the largest and most powerful: for example, Isin, Larsa, Eshnunna, Ashur, Mari and Yamkhad.

Search: Hammurabi, Old Babylonian Period

Chariots up to 25%	Up to a quarter of the units in the army can comprise chariots.
Cavalry up to 1 unit	The army can include a single unit of cavalry representing scouts.
Infantry 75%+	At least three quarters of the units in the army must comprise infantry other than skirmishers.
Light infantry archers 25%+ of infantry	At least one in four non-skirmisher infantry units must be light infantry archers. Light infantry archers include Bai'Irum, Elamite archers and chariot runners.
Divisions 4+ units	Divisions must contain at least 4 units excluding skirmishers, except for cavalry where present, who always form a separate division with their own integral commander. This cavalry division does not count for purposes of breaking the army. All divisions must have a commander.
Skirmishers per division 50% of infantry	Divisions may contain up to half as many skirmisher units as they contain non-skirmisher infantry.

Amorite Babylonian Troop Values

Unit	Clash	Combat Sustained	Short Range	Long Range	Morale Save	Stamina	Special	Points Value
Royal Guard medium infantry with double-handed weapons and throw-sticks – up to 1 unit	7	6	2	0	5+	6	Tough fighters	25 per unit
Sabum Kabitum – medium infantry armed with spears and javelins	6	6	3	0	5+	6		23 per unit
• Replace Sabum Kabitum spears/javelins with long spears (all units or none)	6	6	3/0	0	5+	6		+3 per unit
Sabum Quallatum light infantry armed with spears/javelins or throw-sticks	5	5	3	0	6+	6		20 per unit
• Extra to upgrade one unit of Sabum Quallatum to Bai'Irum with double-handed axes, javelins and bows – up to 1 unit	6	5	3	2	6+	6	Marauders	+6 per unit
Light infantry archers	4	4	3	3	0	6		20 per unit
Light infantry archers as small units	3	3	2	2	0	4		14 per unit
Amorite medium infantry tribal warband with spears, javelins, bows	7	6	2	0	6+	6	Wild fighters	25 per unit
• Reduction to make Amorite warbands levy	7	6	2	0	6+	6	Wild fighters, Levy	-3 per unit
• Amorite warbands may be eager – no more than half number of warbands	7	6	2	0	6+	6	Wild fighters, Eager	Free
Elamite light infantry archers fielded as small units – 1 unit only	4	4	2	2	0	4	Levy, Marauders	16 per unit
Gutian light infantry with double-handed weapons and throw-sticks fielded as small units –1 unit only	5	4	1	0	6+	4	Levy, Marauders	16 per unit
Skirmishers with javelins fielded as small units	3	2	2	0	0	4		11 per unit
Skirmishers with slings fielded as small units	2	2	2	2	0	4		12 per unit
Skirmishers with short bows (range 12") fielded as small units	2	2	2	2	0	4		12 per unit
Light chariots with bow-armed crews	6	6	3	3	4+	6		30 per unit
Chariot runners, light infantry bowmen fielded as a small unit – up to 1 per chariot	3	3	2	2	0	4	Sub-unit with chariot	14 per unit
Cavalry Scouts, bow-armed light cavalry fielded as a small unit – 1 unit only	4	2	1	1	6+	4		15 per unit
Commanders								Free

1 commander must be provided per division.
All commanders including general have leadership 8.

Socketless Axe
New Kingdom Egyptian
c. 1400 BC
(Perry Collection)

THE TRIUMPH OF THE SPARTANS

Herodotus has earned everlasting fame as the father of history and his account of the wars between the Greeks and Persians has coloured many of our views about warfare of the time. Here he describes the Spartan attack upon the Persians at Plataea.

'When some time had elapsed they (the Spartans) advanced against the Persians and the Persians withstood them, laying side their bows. First of all a battle took place about the fence of bucklers; and when that was thrown down, an obstinate fight ensued near the temple of Ceres, and for a long time, till at last they came at a close conflict: for the barbarians laying hold of the enemy's spears, broke them. And indeed, in courage and strength, the Persians were not inferior: but being lightly armed, they were moreover ignorant of military disciple, and not equal to their adversaries in skill; but at rushing forward singly, or in tens, or more or fewer in a body, they fell upon the Spartans and perished.'

Herodotus, *The Histories* (after Cary)

Arabia was a constant source of raiders, mercenaries and settlers from the earliest times onward. This list is good for practically any early desert nomads, not all of whom would have possessed camels or fought from those they had. I've included the stats for those that do.

Search: Shasu, Midianites, Habiru, Apiru.

Infantry 75%+	At least three quarters of the army must be infantry other than skirmishers.
Cavalry up to 25%	Up to a quarter of the units in the army can be camel-mounted cavalry.
Divisions 4+ units	Divisions must contain at least 4 units excluding skirmishers and must be led by a commander.
Skirmishers per division 50% of infantry	Divisions may contain up to half as many skirmisher units as they contain non-skirmisher infantry.

Early Arab Raiders Troop Values

Unit	Combat				Morale Save	Stamina	Special	Points Value
	Clash	Sustained	Short Range	Long Range				
Light infantry archers	4	4	3	3	0	6		20 per unit
Light infantry archers as small units	3	3	2	2	0	4		14 per unit
Light infantry warband with spears and/or javelins	6	5	2	0	6+	6		20 per unit
• *Extra to make warbands eager*	*6*	*5*	*2*	*0*	*6+*	*6*	*Eager*	*Free*
• *Extra to make warband bodyguard – up to 1 unit*	*7*	*5*	*2*	*0*	*6+*	*6*	*Eager, Tough fighters*	*+2 per unit*
Light infantry with javelins	5	5	3	0	6+	6		20 per unit
Skirmishers with javelins fielded as small units	3	2	2	0	0	4		11 per unit
Skirmishers with slings fielded as small units	2	2	2	2	0	4		12 per unit
Skirmishers with short bows (range 12") fielded as a small unit	2	2	2	2	0	4		12 per unit
Camel-mounted light cavalry with javelins	6	5	3	0	6+	6	Feigned flight	27 per unit
Camel-mounted light cavalry with javelins and bows – range 12"	6	5	3	3	6+	6	Feigned flight	30 per unit
Commanders			1 commander must be provided per division. All commanders including general have leadership 8.					Free

Hittite chariots and runners

The Canaanites were a broad group of Semitic peoples who inhabited the region of Syria, Lebanon and Israel otherwise known as the Levant. For our purpose it also covers the cities of northern Syria, such as Ugarit, which were also broadly Semitic, although with some distinctions of language and culture. Canaan was fought over by the Egyptians and Hittites with the cities of Canaan often divided between them. Many of the cities were drawn into the empires of the Mitanni and Hittites.

Search: Phoenicians, Retenu, Amorites, Ugarit, Kadesh, Hazor, Aram.

Chariots 20%+	At least one in five of the units in the army must be chariots.
Infantry 25%+	At least a quarter of the units in the army must be infantry units other than skirmishers.
Cavalry up to 1 unit	The army can include up to one unit of cavalry.
Divisions 4+ units	Divisions must contain at least 4 units excluding skirmishers, except for cavalry where present, who always form a separate division with their own integral commander. This cavalry division does not count for purposes of breaking the army. All divisions must have a commander.
Skirmishers per division 50% of infantry	Divisions may contain up to half as many skirmisher units as they contain non-skirmisher infantry.

Canaanites Troop Values

Unit	Clash	Sustained	Short Range	Long Range	Morale Save	Stamina	Special	Points Value
Canaanite infantry guard with spears and/or javelins – up to 1 unit	6	6	3	0	5+	6	Tough fighters	24 per unit
Canaanite medium infantry with mix of javelins and bows	6	6	3	3	5+	6		26 per unit
Sea Peoples – medium infantry warband with spears and/or javelins	8	6	2	0	5+	6		24 per unit
Canaanite light infantry archers	4	4	3	3	0	6		20 per unit
Habiru light infantry with a mix of javelins and bows fielded as small units	4	4	2	2	0	4		16 per unit
Skirmishers with javelins fielded as small units	3	2	2	0	0	4		11 per unit
Skirmishers with slings fielded as small units	2	2	2	2	0	4		12 per unit
Skirmishers with bows fielded as small units	2	2	2	2	0	4		12 per unit
Light chariots with javelin and bow-armed crews	6	6	3	3	4+	6		30 per unit
Maryannu light chariot with spear and javelin-armed crew – up to 1 unit	8	6	2	0	4+	6	Tough fighters	29 per unit
Chariot runners, light infantry javelinmen fielded as small units – up to 1 unit per chariot	3	3	2	0	6+	4	Sub-unit with chariot	13 per unit
Cavalry scouts, bow-armed light cavalry fielded as small units – up to 1 unit	4	2	1	1	6+	4		15 per unit
Commanders		1 commander must be provided per division. All commanders including general have leadership 8.						Free

> **"The god of war is impartial: he hands out death to the man who hands out death."**
>
> The Iliad

The Hurrian state of Mitanni ruled over an empire that extended into Syria and northern Mesopotamia from its homeland in what is today south-east Turkey. The Hurrians were famed for their horses and chariots. They may well have introduced both into the warfare of the Near East. Many ancient terms used by Hittites, Egyptians and Canaanites for chariot gear and their aristocratic warrior crews are claimed to be derived from the Hurrians. Mitanni grew to become the most powerful Hurrian kingdom after the fall of Babylon to the Hittites and Kassites. The Mitannian empire covered much of northern Mesopotamia and Syria and at that time Mitanni fought with Egypt for control of the Levant.

For a while the empire of the Mitanni was the most powerful of the various northern kingdoms in Mesopotamia. It eventually began to disintegrate under increasing pressure from its neighbours and from civil war within its own borders. The land ruled over by the Mitanni eventually fell to the Assyrians and was divided into a number of successor states including Hanigalbat and Naharin which were drawn into the rival orbits of the Assyrians and Hittites.

Search: Hurrian, Washukanni, Maryannu, Hanigalbat, Naharin.

Chariots 20%+	At least one in five of the units in the army must be chariots.
Infantry 25%+	At least a quarter of the units in the army must be infantry units other that skirmishers.
Cavalry up to 1 unit	The army can include up to one unit of cavalry.
Divisions 4+ units	Divisions must contain at least 4 units excluding skirmishers, except for cavalry where present, who always form a separate division with their own integral commander. This cavalry division does not count for purposes of breaking the army. All divisions must have a commander.
Skirmishers per division 50% of infantry	Divisions may contain up to half as many skirmisher units as they contain non-skirmisher infantry.

Mitanni Troop Values

Unit	Clash	Sustained	Short Range	Long Range	Morale Save	Stamina	Special	Points Value
Hurrian or Syrian medium infantry Shukitukhlu with long spears and shields	6	6	3/0	0	5+	6		26 per unit
Hurrian or Syrian light infantry archers	4	4	3	3	0	6		20 per unit
Phoenician light infantry with a mix of javelins and bows fielded as small units	4	4	2	2	0	4		16 per unit
Habiru light infantry with a mix of javelins and bows fielded as small units	4	4	2	2	0	4		16 per unit
Hupshu light infantry with a mix of javelins and bows fielded as small units	4	4	2	2	0	4	Levy	14 per unit
Skirmishers with javelins fielded as small units	3	2	2	0	0	4		11 per unit
Skirmishers with slings and/or bows (range as slings) fielded as small units	2	2	2	2	0	4		12 per unit
Hurrian light chariots with spear and bow-armed crews	7	6	3	2	4+	6	Tough fighters	31 per unit
• *Uprate Hurrian chariot units to Maryannu – up to half*	7	6	3	2	4+	6	*Tough fighters, Stubborn*	*+3 per unit*
Syrian light chariots with bow and javelin-armed crews	6	6	3	3	4+	6		30 per unit
Chariot runners, light infantry javelinmen fielded as small units – up to 1 unit per chariot	3	3	2	0	6+	4	Sub-unit with chariot	13 per unit
Cavalry scouts, bow-armed light cavalry fielded as a small unit – up to 1 unit	4	2	1	1	6+	4		15 per unit
Commanders								Free

1 commander must be provided per division.
All commanders including general have leadership 8.

The Hittites lived in central Anatolia. At its height their empire extended from the Ionian coast to parts of Syria. They strove to support a string of client states as buffers between the powerful Mitanni to the east and the Egyptians to the south. The Hittites and Egyptians fought to extend their influence over these vassal states. The most famous battle between these two Biblical superpowers was at Kadesh in 1274 BC. The mixed nature of the Hittite forces reflects this system of client kingdoms whose lords were obliged to provide contingents towards the Hittite army. Amongst the vassal states of the Hittites was Wilusa in the far North West – identified with Ilium and the city of Troy.

Search: The Hittite New Kingdom, Musili II, Muwatalli II, The Battle of Kadesh.

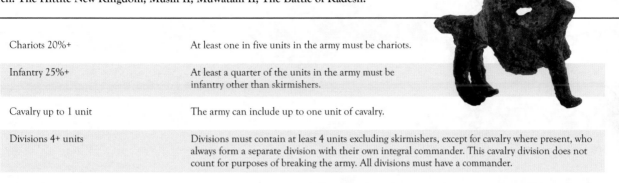

Small bronze
Hittite horseman
Late 2nd millennium BC
(Perry Collection)

Chariots 20%+	At least one in five units in the army must be chariots.
Infantry 25%+	At least a quarter of the units in the army must be infantry other than skirmishers.
Cavalry up to 1 unit	The army can include up to one unit of cavalry.
Divisions 4+ units	Divisions must contain at least 4 units excluding skirmishers, except for cavalry where present, who always form a separate division with their own integral commander. This cavalry division does not count for purposes of breaking the army. All divisions must have a commander.
Skirmishers per division 50% of infantry	Divisions may contain up to half as many skirmisher units as they contain non-skirmisher infantry.

Hittite Troop Values

Unit	Clash	Sustained	Short Range	Long Range	Morale Save	Stamina	Special	Points Value
Hittite, Hurrian, Syrian or Arzawan medium infantry with long spears and shields	6	6	3/0	0	5+	6		26 per unit
Hittite medium infantry guard with double-handed axes – up to 1 unit	7	6	2/0	0	5+	6	Tough fighters	25 per unit
• *Give guard long spears instead of double-handed axes*	6	6	3/0	0	5+	6	*Tough fighters*	*+2 per unit*
Phoenician or Canaanite medium infantry with mix of javelins and bows	6	6	3	3	5+	6		26 per unit
Lukka medium infantry warband	8	6	2	0	5+	6		24 per unit
Hurrian or Syrian light infantry archers	4	4	3	3	0	6		20 per unit
Habiru light infantry with a mix of javelins and bows fielded as small units	4	4	2	2	0	4		16 per unit
Hupshu light infantry with a mix of javelins and bows fielded as small units	4	4	2	2	0	4	Levy	14 per unit
Skirmishers with javelins fielded as small units	3	2	2	0	0	4		11 per unit
• *Extra to give skirmishers slings instead of javelins – up to a half the skirmisher units*	2	2	2	2	0	4		*+1 per unit*
• *Extra to give skirmishers bows instead of javelins – up to quarter the skirmisher units*	2	2	2	2	0	4		*+1 per unit*
Light chariots with spear and javelin-armed crews	8	6	2	0	4+	6		28 per unit
• *Uprate Chariot unit to Maryannu – up to 1 unit*	8	6	2	0	4+	6	*Tough fighters*	*+1 pt per unit*
Hittite chariot runners, light infantry javelinmen fielded as a small unit – up to 1 per chariot	3	3	2	0	6+	4	Sub-unit with chariot	13 per unit
Cavalry Scouts, bow-armed light cavalry fielded as a small unit – up to 1 unit	4	2	1	1	6+	4		15 per unit
• *Uprate Scouts to spear-armed light cavalry*	5	3	2	0	6+	4		*+2 per unit*
Commanders								Free

1 commander must be provided per division.
All commanders including general have leadership 8.

This list represents the final phases of Minoan civilisation once Crete had fallen to Greek speaking invaders – it might therefore equally well be described as an Helladic or Achaean list covering the early Greek city states of the Aegean region. Some scholars identify the Cretans and surrounding Aegean islands with the Sea Peoples who invaded Egypt and the Levant in the time of Rameses III. The Hyksos pharoahs of Avaris built palaces decorated in Minoan style and the last (Great Hyksos) arguably have Greek names. Note that the Lukka were notorious pirates and raiders from what was to become the region of Lycia in Anatolia.

Search: Mycenae, Tiryns, Knossos, The Achaeans, The Late Helladic Period.

Chariots up to 25%	Up to a quarter of the units in the army can be chariots.
Infantry 75%+	At least three quarters of the units in the army must be infantry other than skirmishers.
Mycenaean or Minoan medium infantry 25% of infantry	At least a quarter of the non-skirmisher infantry units in the army must be Mycenaean or Minoan medium infantry units of one kind or other.
Divisions 4+ units	Divisions must contain at least 4 units excluding skirmishers and be led by a commander.
Skirmishers per division 50% of infantry	Divisions may contain up to half as many skirmisher units as they contain non-skirmisher infantry.

Mycenaean Troop Values

Unit	Clash	Sustained	Short Range	Long Range	Morale Save	Stamina	Special	Points Value
Mycenaean or Minoan medium infantry with long spears	6	6	3/0	0	5+	6		26 per unit
Mycenaean or Minoan medium infantry with mixed long spears and bows	6	6	3	1	5+	6		27 per unit
Mycenaean or Minoan medium infantry with javelins and shields	6	6	3	0	5+	6		23 per unit
Royal Guard medium infantry with double-handed axes – up to 1 unit	7	6	0/2	0	5+	6	Tough fighters	25 per unit
Mycenaean or Minoan light infantry archers fielded as small units	3	3	2	2	6+	4		15 per unit
Mycenaean or Minoan light infantry javelinmen fielded as small units	3	3	2	0	6+	4		13 per unit
Chariot runners light infantry javelinmen fielded as small units – up to 1 unit per chariot	3	3	2	0	6+	4	Sub-unit with chariot	13 per unit
Skirmishers armed with javelins or hand-hurled stones, fielded as small units	3	2	2	0	0	4	Levy	9 per unit
Skirmishers armed with slings or with mixed slings and bows (range as slings) fielded as small units	2	2	2	2	0	4	Levy	10 per unit
Lukka medium infantry mercenary warband armed with swords and javelins	8	6	2	0	5+	6		24 per unit
Light chariots with spear and javelin-armed crews	8	6	2	0	4+	6		28 per unit
Commanders		1 commander must be provided per division. All commanders including general have leadership 8.						Free

"Heaven cannot brook two suns, nor earth two masters."

Alexander the Great

NEW KINGDOM EGYPTIAN

This list represents the armies of ancient Egypt at its height during the 18th, 19th and 20th dynasties when Egypt battled for control of the Levant with the Canaanites, Mitanni and Hittites. This is the period associated with Ramesses, Tutankhamun and the heretic pharoah Akhenaten. The Libyan and Kushite archer units can have a mix of weapons and not just bows. Use the archer stat given for these. Skirmishers can be Egyptians or any subject race, including Nubians, who were likely to be bow-armed. Slingers were often Arabs. The cavalry scouts have been given a deliberately reduced stat line to reflect the general lack of capability of these early horsemen. The Ne'Arin was an elite unit of chariots that fought at the battle of Kadesh.

Search: The 18th, 19th and 20th Dynasties, The Amarna period, the Ramesside period, The Battle of Megiddo, the Battle of Kadesh.

Chariots up to 25%	Up to a quarter of the units in the army can be chariots.
Infantry 75%+	At least three quarters of the units in the army must be infantry other than skirmishers.
Egyptian medium infantry 50%+ of infantry	At least half of the non-skirmish infantry in the army must be specifically Egyptian medium infantry of one kind or other.
Cavalry up to 1 unit	The army can include a single unit of cavalry representing scouts.
Divisions 4+ units	Divisions must contain at least 4 units excluding skirmishers, except for cavalry where present, who always form a separate division with their own integral commander. This cavalry division does not count for purposes of breaking the army. All divisions must have a commander.
Skirmishers per division 50% of infantry	Divisions may contain up to half as many skirmisher units as they contain non-skirmisher infantry.

New Kingdom Egyptian Troop Values

Unit	Combat				Morale Save	Stamina	Special	Points Value
	Clash	Sustained	Short Range	Long Range				
Egyptian medium infantry with spears and shields	6	6	3	0	5+	6		23 per unit
Egyptian medium infantry with double-handed mace-axes	7	6	2/0	0	5+	6		24 per unit
Egyptian medium infantry archers	5	5	3	3	5+	6		24 per unit
Egyptian marines – medium infantry	7	7	3	0	5+	6	Tough fighters	26 per unit
• *Extra to field Egyptian marines as mixed units of bows and javelins*	7	7	3	3	5+	6	*Tough fighters*	+3 per unit
Sherden guard, medium infantry – up to 1 unit	7	7	3	0	5+	6	Elite, Stubborn	30 per unit
Sea Peoples – medium infantry warband	8	6	2	0	5+	6		24 per unit
Libyan, Syrian or Kushite light infantry	5	5	3	0	6+	6		20 per unit
Libyan, Syrian or Kushite light infantry archers	4	4	3	3	0	6		20 per unit
Skirmishers with javelins fielded as small units	3	2	2	0	0	4		11 per unit
• *Extra to give skirmishers slings instead of javelins – up to a quarter the skirmisher units*	2	2	2	2	0	4		+1 per unit
• *Extra to give skirmishers bows instead of javelins – up to half the skirmisher units*	2	2	2	2	0	4		+1 per unit
Light chariots with bow-armed crews	6	6	3	3	4+	6		30 per unit
Ne'Arin light chariots with spear-armed crews – up to 1 unit	8	6	2	0	4+	6	Tough fighters	29 per unit
Egyptian chariot runners, light infantry javelinmen fielded as small units – up to 1 unit per chariot	3	3	2	0	6+	4	Sub-unit with chariot	13 per unit
Cavalry scouts, bow-armed light cavalry fielded as a small unit – up to 1 unit	4	2	1	1	6+	4		15 per unit
Commanders	1 commander must be provided per division. All commanders including general have leadership 8.							Free

This army represents the re-emergent kings of what historians call the Middle Assyrian period. Assyrian chariots started to become more robust and were often pulled by three or even four horses during the 9th century BC. Prior to that chariots were drawn by two horses in the same fashion as in Hittite, Hurrian, and other contemporary armies. I have made these new types of chariot 'stubborn', making them half-way between light and heavy chariots. At the same time, the Assyrians started to develop a cavalry arm, represented here by the light and medium cavalry entries. Earlier cavalry would have been restricted to a scouting role. Initially these cavalry operated in pairs, one man to hold the horses whilst the other shot his bow. The light infantry levy are intended to represent troops from subjugated territories enrolled to serve as auxiliaries. These could be from any of the regions under Assyrian rule. From the 9th century BC they would include Aramaeans and Neo-Hittites.

Search: Ashur-uballit I, Shalmaneser I, Tiglath-Peleser I, Battle of Qarqar, Battle of Nihriya.

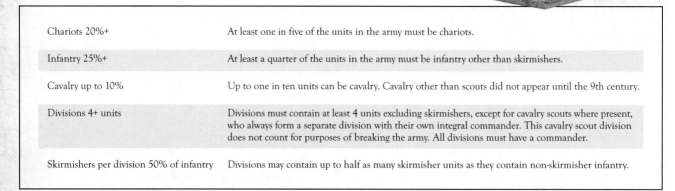

Chariots 20%+	At least one in five of the units in the army must be chariots.			
Infantry 25%+	At least a quarter of the units in the army must be infantry other than skirmishers.			
Cavalry up to 10%	Up to one in ten units can be cavalry. Cavalry other than scouts did not appear until the 9th century.			
Divisions 4+ units	Divisions must contain at least 4 units excluding skirmishers, except for cavalry scouts where present, who always form a separate division with their own integral commander. This cavalry scout division does not count for purposes of breaking the army. All divisions must have a commander.			
Skirmishers per division 50% of infantry	Divisions may contain up to half as many skirmisher units as they contain non-skirmisher infantry.			

Early Assyrian Troop Values

Unit	Clash	Sustained	Short Range	Long Range	Morale Save	Stamina	Special	Points Value
Asharruti medium infantry with mixed spears and bows, and/or slings	6	6	3	3	5+	6		26 per unit
• Extra to upgrade Asharruti to elite	6	6	3	3	5+	6	Elite	+3 *per unit*
• Extra to upgrade Asharruti to armoured medium infantry – up to 1 unit	6	6	3	3	4+	6	Elite	+4 *per unit*
Hupshu light infantry with a mix of javelins and bows fielded as small units	4	4	2	2	0	4		16 per unit
Light infantry levy with javelins	5	5	3	0	6+	6	Levy	17 per unit
Skirmishers with javelins fielded as small units	3	2	2	0	0	4		11 per unit
Skirmishers with slings fielded as small units	2	2	2	2	0	4		12 per unit
Skirmishers with bows fielded as small units	2	2	2	2	0	4		12 per unit
Assyrian two-horse light chariots with bow and javelin-armed crews	6	6	3	3	4+	6		30 per unit
Assyrian three or four-horse light chariots with bow and javelin-armed crews	6	6	3	3	4+	6	Stubborn	33 per unit
Chariot runners, light infantry javelinmen fielded as small units – up to one per chariot	3	3	2	0	6+	4	Sub-unit with chariot	13 per unit
Cavalry Scouts, bow-armed light cavalry fielded as a small unit – up to 1 unit	4	2	1	1	6+	4		15 per unit
Assyrian light cavalry with mix of spears and bows	5	5	2	2	6+	6		24 per unit
Assyrian medium cavalry with spears and/or javelins	6	5	3	0	5+	6		25 per unit
Commanders	1 commander must be provided per division. All commanders including general have leadership 8.							Free

This is a fairly speculative list by nature, since the people of the time have left no record beyond the cold and mute remains exposed by archaeology. So, what we have here is a reconstruction based on later armies to produce what I intend to be a credible model of earlier warfare, with light infantry warbands forming the chief components of armies focussed on raiding and feuding. The weapons chosen reflect archaeological finds whilst the use of chariots is inferred from finds of carts and wagons as well as later practice. Plainly this is a list that could be framed differently and expanded almost indefinitely with any number of colourful and entertaining warriors.

Search: The Atlantic Bronze Age, Nordic Bronze Age, Central European Bronze Age, The Urnfield Culture.

Warriors of the North European Bronze Age assault a fortified village.

Infantry 75%+	At least three quarters of the units in the army must be infantry other than skirmishers.
Chariots up to 10%	Up to one in ten units in the army can be chariots.
Divisions 4+ units	Divisions must contain at least 4 units excluding skirmishers, unless they comprise chariots, or chariots and runner sub-units only, in which case they can be any size. Each division must be led by a commander.
Skirmishers per division 50% of infantry	Divisions may contain up to half as many skirmisher units as they contain non-skirmisher infantry.

North European Bronze Age Troop Values

Unit	Clash	Sustained	Short Range	Long Range	Morale Save	Stamina	Special	Points Value
Light infantry warband with mixed arms	8	5	2	0	6+	6		22 per unit
• *Reduction to field light infantry warbands as small units*	6	3	1	0	6+	4		-7 per unit
Medium infantry chieftain's warband fielded as a small unit – up to 1 unit	7	4	1	0	5+	4	Tough fighters, Stubborn	21 per unit
• *Extra to field the chieftain's warband with double-handed axes*	8	4	1/0	0	5+	4	*Tough fighters, Stubborn*	+2 per unit
Skirmishers with javelins fielded as small units	3	2	2	0	0	4		11 per unit
Skirmishers with slings fielded as small units	2	2	2	2	0	4		12 per unit
Skirmishers with bows fielded as a small unit – up to 1 unit	2	2	2	2	0	4		12 per unit
Light chariots with mix-armed crews	6	5	3	0	4+	6		26 per unit
Chariot runners, light infantry with javelins fielded as small units - up to 1 per chariot unit	3	3	2	0	0	4	Sub-unit with chariot	12 per unit
Commanders								Free

1 commander must be provided per division.
All commanders including general have leadership 8.

The barbarian tribes of Libya formed the chief western threat to Egypt throughout much of its early history. The Libyans allied with the Sea Peoples to attack Egypt in the time of Rameses III. The Libyans themselves were not hugely dissimilar to the Egyptians in terms of their skin tones – they were probably the autochthonous Berbers of north Africa. This list covers a long time period and overlaps with some of the Classical lists. For this reason I have included two-horse and four-horse light chariots as well as heavy chariots. Two-horse chariots fell out of use and were replaced by four-horse chariots at about the same time this happened elsewhere – so armies should really include one or the other and not both. I've treated four-horse chariots as light rather than heavy, as I can't see them as lumbering wagons given the general nature of the army. A later army – up until the Roman annexation – can be made by replacing chariots with light cavalry armed with javelins along the lines of Numidians. See the Numidian list for suitable examples of these.

Search: Libu, Meshwesh, Berbers, Sea Peoples Alliance.

Infantry up to 75%+	At least three quarters of the units in the army must be infantry other than skirmishers.
Light infantry javelins 50%+ of infantry	At least half of the non-skirmish infantry units must be light infantry with javelins of one kind or other.
Chariots up to 25%	Up to a quarter of the units in the army can be chariots.
Divisions 4+ units	Divisions must contain at least 4 units excluding skirmishers and must be led by a commander. Guard must form part of the general's division.
Skirmishers per division 50% of infantry	Divisions may contain up to half as many skirmisher units as they contain non-skirmisher infantry.

Libyan Troop Values

Unit	Clash	Sustained	Short Range	Long Range	Morale Save	Stamina	Special	Points Value
Libyan light infantry warband with javelins	7	5	2	0	6+	6		21 per unit
• Extra to give warbands mixed javelins and bows	7	5	2	1	6+	6		+1 per unit
• Extra to make either of the above chieftain's guard – up to 1 unit			— As above —				Tough fighters, Stubborn	+2 per unit
• Extra to make any of the above wild fighters			— As above —				As above +Wild fighters	+3 per unit
Light infantry with javelins	5	5	3	0	0	6		19 per unit
Light infantry with bows	4	4	3	3	0	6		20 per unit
• Reduction to field light infantry with bows as small units	3	3	2	2	0	4		-6 per unit
Skirmishers with javelins fielded as small units	3	2	2	0	0	4		11 per unit
• Extra to give skirmishers bows instead of javelins – up to half	2	2	2	2	0	4		+1 pt per unit
Two-horse light chariots with javelin-armed crews	6	6	3	0	4+	6		27 per unit
Four-horse light chariots with javelin-armed crews	8	6	3	0	4+	6		29 per unit
Commanders		1 commander must be provided per division. The general has leadership 8. All other commanders have leadership 7.						Free

Greek hoplite phalanx

The various tribes known to the Egyptians as The Sea Peoples wrought havoc throughout the eastern Mediterranean and settled into the southern Levant. The Sherden allied with the Libyans and attacked Egypt from the west. After their defeat the Sherden were incorporated into the guard of the pharaoh. The Lukka probably came from Lycia in the South West of Anatolia – they were notorious and skilled pirates into later times. The Philistines are probably to be identified with the Peleset who settled into the southern Levant after their defeat by Rameses III. Their name is recorded in several Egyptian sources, most notably at the mortuary temple of Rameses at Medinet Habu. Exactly where the Sea Peoples came from is a bit of a mystery. Favourites are eastern Anatolia, the Islands of the Aegean, and mainland Greece.

Search: Bronze Age Collapse, Lukka, Sherden, Ekwesh, Skekelesh, Teresh, Peleset, Tjeker, Denyen, Pharaoh Merneptah's Battle Against the Sea People, The Battle of the Delta, The Battle of Djahy.

Chariots up to 25%	Up to a quarter of the units in the army can be chariots.
Infantry 75%+	At least three quarters of units in the army must be infantry other than skirmishers.
Baggage wagons 1-3	The army must include at least 1 unit of baggage wagons and may have up to 3. A unit is one wagon.
Divisions 4+ units.	Divisions must contain at least 4 units and be led by a commander. Baggage wagons must all be included in the same division – the loss of the baggage wagons must surely result in immediate defeat! Libyans must be fielded in their own divisions – Libyans can include chariot runners and skirmishers as noted below.
Skirmishers per division 50% of infantry	Divisions may contain up to half as many skirmisher units as they contain non-skirmisher infantry.

Sea Peoples Troop Values

Unit	Clash	Sustained	Short Range	Long Range	Morale Save	Stamina	Special	Points Value
Sea Peoples – medium infantry warband with swords and javelins	8	6	2	0	5+	6		24 per unit
• Extra to make Sea Peoples Warband Lukka Pirates – up to 1 in 4 units	8	6	2	0	5+	6	Wild fighters	+3 per unit
• Extra to make Sea Peoples Warband Sherden Swordsmen – up to 1 in 4 units	8	6	2	0	5+	6	Tough fighters Stubborn	+3 per unit
• Extra to include a proportion of bowmen into rear ranks of warbands not upgraded to Lukka or Sherden	8	6	2	1	5+	6		+1 per unit
• Extra to make any of the above warbands eager			As above				As above + eager	Free
Libyan light infantry warband with mixed javelins and bows	7	5	2	1	6+	6		22 per unit
• Extra to make Libyan warband tough fighters – up to 1 unit	7	5	2	1	6+	6	Tough fighters	+1 per unit
Sea Peoples or Libyan light infantry with bows	4	4	3	3	0	6		20 per unit
Sea Peoples or Libyan light infantry with bows fielded as small units	3	3	2	2	0	4		14 per unit
Skirmishers with javelins fielded as small units	3	2	2	0	0	4		11 per unit
Skirmishers with bows fielded as small units	2	2	2	2	0	4		12 per unit
Sea People two-horse light chariots with spear and javelin-armed crews	8	6	2	0	4+	6		28 per unit
• Extra to upgrade Sea People light chariots to tough fighters – up to 1 unit	8	6	2	0	4+	6	Tough fighters	+1 per unit
Libyan two-horse light chariots with javelin-armed crews	6	5	3	0	4+	6		26 per unit
Chariot runners, light infantry javelinmen fielded as small units – up to 1 per chariot	3	3	2	0	6+	4	Sub-unit with chariot	13 per unit
Baggage wagon with womenfolk and armed guards	3	3	1	0	4+	6	Stubborn	Free
Commanders		1 commander must be provided per division. All commanders including general have leadership 8.						Free

This list represents the armies of the emergent united land of Israel under the House of David. The new kingdom flourished under Solomon, who built up the new nation's armies and especially its chariotry. Under his successor Rehoboam the land was divided into the two kingdoms of Israel and Judeah, and its influence much diminished. In the north the Assyrians eventually conquered Israel in 720 BC. In the south Judeah endured until conquered by the Neo-Babylonians in 586 BC. The different tribes of Israel have been given different weapons and qualities based upon what we know of their preferred tactics and upon their reputation amongst the other tribes. Obviously to some extent these are speculative and perhaps should not be taken too literally but do add colour and interest to the army.

Search: Saul, David, Solomon, The Capture of Jerusalem from the Jebusites.

Chariots 25%+	At least a quarter of the units in the army must be chariots.
Infantry 50%+	At least a half of the units in the army must be infantry other than skirmishers..
Cavalry	Cavalry outriders can be included as sub-units of chariots as noted. Camel riders are restricted to a single unit.
Divisions 4+ units	Divisions must contain at least 4 units excluding skirmishers and must be led by a commander.
Skirmishers per division 50% of infantry	Divisions may contain up to half as many skirmisher units as they contain non-skirmisher infantry.

Israel and Judean Troop Values

Unit	Combat				Morale Save	Stamina	Special	Points Value
	Clash	Sustained	Short Range	Long Range				
Gibborim guard medium infantry armed with spears and javelins – up to 1 unit	6	6	3	0	5+	6	Stubborn, Tough fighters	26 per unit
Judean spearmen medium infantry with spears and shields	6	6	3	0	5+	6		23 per unit
Gadite light infantry with javelins	5	5	3	0	0	6		19 per unit
Zebulunite light infantry with mix of spears and bows	5	5	3	3	0	6		22 per unit
Danite light infantry sword-and-buckler men	5	5	0/3	0	6+	6	Tough fighters	21 per unit
Benjamite light infantry with slings or mixed slings and bows (range: slings) fielded as small units	3	3	2	2	0	4	Marksmen	15 per unit
Issachar skirmishers with javelins fielded as small units	3	2	2	0	0	4		11 per unit
Issachar skirmishers with bows fielded as small units	2	2	2	2	0	4		12 per unit
Philistine medium infantry with swords and javelins – up to 1 unit	6	6	3	0	5+	6	Tough fighters	24 per unit
Phoenician medium infantry with javelins and bows – up to 1 unit	6	6	3	3	5+	6		26 per unit
Edomite, Moabite, or Ammonite skirmishers with javelins fielded as small units	3	2	2	0	0	4		11 per unit
Arab camel-riding light cavalry armed with bows fielded as a small unit – up to 1 unit	5	3	2	2	6+	4	Feigned flight	21 per unit
Light chariots with bow and spear-armed crews	7	6	3	2	4+	6		30 per unit
Ne'arim light chariots with bow and spear-armed crews – up to 1 unit	7	6	3	2	4+	6	Tough fighters	31 per unit
Chariot runners, light infantry javelinmen fielded as small units – up to 1 unit per chariot	3	3	2	0	6+	4	Sub-unit with chariot	13 per unit
Cavalry outriders, light cavalry spearmen fielded as small units – up to 1 unit per chariot	5	3	2	0	6+	4	Sub-unit with chariot	17 per unit

Commanders	1 commander must be provided per division. All commanders including general have leadership 8.	Free
• Extra to upgrade general with Ark of the Covenant.	*The Ark of the Covenant can be borne by the general's entourage as an army standard, in which case his leadership is increased to 9 and any unit he has joined becomes valiant whilst he remains with it.*	+25

This list represents the armies of Assyria during the Iron Age after the reforms of King Tiglath-Pileser III. At this time Assyria controlled an empire that included Egypt as well as most of the Near East. During this period the Assyrians replaced the light chariots with effective cavalry supported by larger and heavier chariots. Four-horse chariots were in use by the reign of Ashurnasirpal (685-627 BC). Kallipani are infantry mounted on carts. They are represented by light infantry and a number of cart models; we suggest three. So long as the unit is more than 12" from the enemy and is moving over terrain that would otherwise be accessible to chariots/carts the unit moves at 9" rather than 6". If enemy are within 12" or the unit is moving over terrain unsuitable for vehicles its movement is reduced to 6" and if the unit moves into terrain through which carts cannot pass they must be abandoned. It is not necessary to actually mount the infantry into carts for moving – it is enough that the carts are present – but players who wish to do so can provide cart-mounted models to substitute for their infantry.

Search: Tiglath-Pileser III, the Sargonid dynasty, Ashurbanipal, Syrian-Ephramite War, Urartu-Assyrian War.

Cavalry and Chariots up to 25%	Up to a quarter of the units in the army can be cavalry or chariots. Note that Kallipani count as infantry.
Cavalry 50%+ of mounted	At least half of the cavalry and chariot units must be cavalry.
Infantry 75%+	At least three quarters of the units in the army must be infantry other than skirmishers.
Kisir Sharruti 25%+	At least a quarter of the non-skirmisher infantry units in the army must be Kisir Sharruti, and units equipped with slings and bows must not outnumber those equipped with spears and bows.
Sab Sharri/Kallipani 25%+	At least a quarter of the non-skirmisher infantry units in the army must be Sab Sharri or Kallipani.
Divisions 4+ units	Divisions must contain at least 4 units excluding skirmishers and must be led by a commander.
Skirmishers per division 50% of infantry	Divisions may contain up to half as many skirmisher units as they contain non-skirmisher infantry.

Assyrian Empire Troop Values

Unit	Clash	Sustained	Short Range	Long Range	Morale Save	Stamina	Special	Points Value
Kisir Sharruti medium infantry with mixed spears and bows	6	6	3	3	5+	6	Stubborn, Tough fighters	29 per unit
• Extra to upgrade Kisir Sharruti to Qurubuti Royal Guard with spears and shields – 1 unit only	7	7	3	0	5+	6	Stubborn, Tough fighters, Steady	+2 per unit
Kisir Sharruti medium infantry with mixed bows and slings (range as bows)	5	5	3	3	5+	6	Marksmen	25 per unit
Sab Sharri light infantry with mixed spears and bows	5	5	3	3	6+	6		23 per unit
Kallipani bow-armed light infantry on carts – up to 1 unit	4	4	3	3	0	6	Marksmen (see notes above)	24 per unit
Phrygian or Mannaean medium infantry with long spears	6	6	3/0	0	5+	6		26 per unit
Elamite light infantry with bows – up to 1 unit	4	4	3	3	0	6	Levy	17 per unit
Aramaean or Chaldean skirmishers with javelins fielded as small units	3	2	2	0	0	4		11 per unit
Aramaean, Arab or Chaldean skirmishers with slings or bows (range as slings) fielded as small units	2	2	2	2	0	4		12 per unit
Arab camel-riding light cavalry armed with bows fielded as a small unit – 1 unit only	5	3	2	2	6+	4	Feigned flight	21 per unit
Medium cavalry with mixed spears and bows	8	5	3	2	5+	6		29 per unit
Royal Guard heavy cavalry with spears and bows riding barded horses – 1 unit only	9	6	3	2	4+	6	Steady	35 per unit
Four-horse heavy chariots with crews armed with bows, spears and javelins	9	5	3	3	3+	6		33 per unit
Commanders		1 commander must be provided per division. All commanders including general have leadership 8.						Free

This is the army of the resurgent Babylonians who, allied with Medes and Scythians, overthrew the Assyrians and sacked Nineveh in 612 BC. The rulers of this period are known as the Chaldean dynasty – Chaldea being the region around Babylon as well as the name of its principal tribe. Babylonia had always been an unruly province under the Assyrian empire. When Assyria started to disintegrate after the death of Ashurbanipal the Babylonians rose up against them and in the new order that emerged, the Babylonians became the major power in the Near East, battling against Egypt for control of the old Assyrian provinces that lay between them. The Babylonian hold upon power was relatively short-lived however, with Babylon falling to the Persians under Cyrus the Great in 539 BC.

The Neo-Babylonian army has much in common with the late Assyrian army. Elamites riding carts are represented by light infantry and a number of cart models – we suggest three. So long as the unit is more than 12" from the enemy and is moving over terrain that would otherwise be accessible to chariots/carts the unit moves at 9" rather than 6". If enemy are within 12", or the unit is moving over terrain unsuitable for vehicles, its movement is reduced to 6" and if the unit moves into terrain through which carts cannot pass they have to be abandoned. It is not necessary to actually mount the infantry into carts for moving – it is enough that the carts are present – but players who wish to do so can provide cart-mounted models to substitute for their infantry.

Search: Chaldean, Nabopolassar, Nebuchadnezzar.

Cavalry and Chariots up to 25%	Up to a quarter of the units in the army can be cavalry or chariots.
Infantry 75%+	At least three quarters of the units in the army must be infantry other than skirmishers.
Kisir 1+ units	The army must include at least one unit of Babylonian Kisir.
Divisions 4+ units	Divisions must contain at least 4 units excluding skirmishers and must be led by a commander.
Skirmishers per division 50% of infantry	Divisions may contain up to half as many skirmisher units as they contain non-skirmisher infantry.

Neo-Babylonian Troop Values

Unit	Clash	Sustained	Short Range	Long Range	Morale Save	Stamina	Special	Points Value
Babylonian Kisir medium infantry with mixed spears and bows	6	6	3	3	5+	6		26 per unit
Mede medium infantry armed with spears and bows – up to 1 unit.	6	6	3	3	5+	6		26 per unit
Sab Sharri or Chaldean light infantry with mixed spears and bows	5	5	3	3	6+	6		23 per unit
Chaldean light infantry with spears and shields	5	5	3	0	6+	6		20 per unit
Chaldean or Elamite light infantry with bows	4	4	3	3	6+	6		21 per unit
• *Extra to provide Elamites with carts*	4	4	3	3	6+	6	(See notes above)	+3 *per unit*
Greek or Lydian heavy infantry hoplites with long spears – up to 1 unit	7	7	0/3	0	4+	6	Phalanx	32 per unit
Aramaean or Chaldean skirmishers with javelins fielded as small units	3	2	2	0	0	4		11 per unit
Aramaean, Arab or Chaldean skirmishers with slings or bows (range as slings) fielded as small units	2	2	2	2	0	4		12 per unit
Arab camel-riding light cavalry armed with bows fielded as small units	5	3	2	2	6+	4	Feigned flight	21 per unit
Babylonian medium cavalry with mixed spears and bows	8	5	3	2	5+	6		29 per unit
Scythian horse archers fielded as small units	4	2	2	2	6+	4	Parthian shot	19 per unit
Elamite light cavalry with spears and bows	7	5	3	3	6+	6		28 per unit
Babylonian or Urartian four-horse heavy chariots with crew armed with bows, spears and javelins	9	5	3	3	3+	6		33 per unit
Commanders								Free

1 commander must be provided per division.
All commanders including general have leadership 8.

The Kingdom of Urartu in the Armenian highlands was the northern neighbour of the Assyrians. Urartu was the successor to the Mitanni Kingdom of the Late Bronze Age. It flourished from the mid-ninth century and was conquered by the Medes (590 BC). Urartu fought against the Assyrians and the Cimmerians. Its armies were similar to Assyria and are represented along the same mixed model. Stats for separately armed units are given as an option. Kallipani are represented by light infantry and cart models (3). So long as the unit is more than 12" from the enemy and is moving over terrain that would otherwise be accessible to chariots/carts the unit moves at 9" rather than 6". If enemy are within 12" or the unit is moving over terrain unsuitable for vehicles its movement is reduced to 6" and if the unit moves into terrain through which carts cannot pass they must be abandoned. It is not necessary to actually mount the infantry into carts for moving – it is enough that the carts are present. Players who wish can provide cart-mounted models to substitute for infantry. I have included stats for Cimmerian horse archers as they allied with the Urartians, though they are commonly found as foes of Urartu or even allies of Assyria.

Search: Urartu, Ararat, Kingdom of Van, Tushpa, Urartu-Assyrian War, The Two Battles of Arpad 754 and 743 BC, Sarduri son of Argišti.

Cavalry and Chariots up to 25%	Up to a quarter of the units in the army can be cavalry or chariots. Note that Kallipani count as infantry.
Cavalry 50%+ of mounted	At least half of the cavalry and chariot units must be cavalry other than allied Cimmerians.
Infantry 75%+	At least three quarters of the units in the army must be infantry other than skirmishers.
Urartian medium infantry 25%+	At least a quarter of the non-skirmisher infantry units in the army must be Urartian medium infantry. This includes any units upgraded to Qurubuti.
Divisions 4+ units	Divisions must contain at least 4 units excluding skirmishers and must be led by a commander.
Skirmishers per division 50% of infantry	Divisions may contain up to half as many skirmisher units as they contain non-skirmisher infantry.

Urartu Troop Values

Unit	Clash	Sustained	Short Range	Long Range	Morale Save	Stamina	Special	Points Value
Urartian medium infantry with mixed spears and bows	6	6	3	3	5+	6		26 per unit
• *Extra to upgrade Urartian medium infantry to Qurubuti – up to half*	6	6	3	3	5+	6	*Stubborn, Tough fighters.*	*+3 per unit*
Urartian medium infantry with spears	6	6	3	0	5+	6		23 per unit
• *Extra to make Urartian medium infantry guards with double-handed axes – up to 1 unit*	8	7	2/0	0	5+	6	*Stubborn, Tough fighters, Steady*	*+9 per unit*
Urartian light infantry with mixed spears and bows	5	5	3	3	6+	6		23 per unit
Urartian light infantry with spears	5	5	3	0	6+	6		20 per unit
Urartian light infantry with bows	4	4	3	3	0	6		20 per unit
Kallipani bow-armed light infantry on carts – up to 1 unit	4	4	3	3	0	6	Marksmen (see notes above)	24 per unit
Phrygian or Mannaean medium infantry with long spears	6	6	3/0	0	5+	6		26 per unit
Aramaean or Highland skirmishers with javelins fielded as small units	3	2	2	0	0	4		11 per unit
Aramaean or Highland skirmishers with slings or bows (range as slings) fielded as small units	2	2	2	2	0	4		12 per unit
Medium cavalry with mixed spears and bows	8	5	3	2	5+	6		29 per unit
Royal Guard heavy cavalry with spears and bows riding barded horses – up to 1 unit	9	6	3	2	4+	6	Steady	35 per unit
Four-horse heavy chariots with crews armed with bows, spears and javelins	9	5	3	3	3+	6		33 per unit
Allied Cimmerian horse archers as small units	4	2	2	2	6+	4	Parthian shot	19 per unit
Commanders		1 commander must be provided per division. All commanders including general have leadership 8.						Free

The Scythians were nomadic people who lived upon the Pontic-Caspian steppe. In ancient times this region was known as Scythia or Sarmatia. The Scythians spoke an Indo-European language and were closely related to the Persians and Parthians – all noted horsemen and archers. Scythian tribes lived around the mouth of the Danube in the west and as far as Bactria and the Indus valley in the east. They were possibly amongst the first people to domesticate the horse and develop wheeled wagons. Later writers continue to use the term Scythians for all kinds of steppe peoples. Of these the Sarmatians, Alani, Iazyges, Aorsi, Siraces, and Roxalani are almost certainly the same people previously referred to as Scythians. The strength of the Scythians is in their cavalry and specifically in the horse archers that make up the bulk of the army. I have described the horse archers as small units as I find this best represents this troop type overall and looks attractive on the tabletop. A small cadre of heavy armoured cavalry represent members of the ruling warrior caste and is limited in number as you see. The majority of the infantry represent troops provided by settled subjects from areas conquered by the Scythians, although some Scythians may also have fought on foot as archers or skirmishers. In Europe such infantry may have included troops from the Greek colonies of the Crimea as well as Thracian tribes west of the Black Sea, some of whom fought as mercenaries during Atheios' war against Philip of Macedon. For this reason I have included the option to field a reasonable number of infantry, including tribal levy, but note that it is entirely possible to field an entirely mounted army as may be more representative of Scythians on the Pontic Steppe.

Search: Scythia, Cimmerians, King Atheios, Battle of Jaxartes, Saka, Dahae, Massagetae, Issyk Kurgan.

Cavalry 75%+	At least three quarters of the units in the army must be cavalry.
Horse Archers 75%+ of cavalry	At least three quarters of the cavalry units in the army must be horse archers.
Infantry up to 25%	Up to a quarter of the units in the army can be infantry other than skirmishers.
Divisions 4+ units	Divisions must contain at least 4 units excluding skirmishers and must be led by a commander.
Skirmishers per division 50% of infantry	Divisions may contain up to half as many skirmisher units as they contain non-skirmisher infantry.

Scythian Troop Values

Unit	Clash	Sustained	Short Range	Long Range	Morale Save	Stamina	Special	Points Value
Heavy cavalry armed with kontos and bows – up to 3 units	9	6	3	2	4+	6		35 per unit
Horse archers fielded as small units	4	2	2	2	6+	4	Parthian shot	19 per unit
Light cavalry armed with spears/javelins and bows fielded as small units	5	3	2	2	6+	4	Feigned flight	21 per unit
Subject or tribal medium infantry with javelins and/or spears	6	6	3	0	5+	6	Levy	20 per unit
Light infantry archers	4	4	3	3	0	6		20 per unit
• *Reduction to field light infantry archers as small units*	3	3	2	2	0	4		*–6 per unit*
Light infantry armed with javelins and/or spears	5	5	3	0	0	6		19 per unit
• *Reduction to field light infantry with spear/javelins as small units*	4	4	2	0	0	4		*–5 per unit*
Skirmishers with javelins fielded as small units	3	2	2	0	0	4		11 per unit
Skirmishers with bows fielded as small units	2	2	2	2	0	4		12 per unit
Commanders	1 commander must be provided per division. All commanders including general have leadership 8.							Free

> *"Of that whole army which fought and fled, not a single free-born citizen was taken prisoner: all were as careless of their own as of the enemies' lives."*
>
> Sallust, *The Conspiracy of Cataline*

THE ROMANS IN IRELAND

For many years it was assumed that the Romans never made it as far as Ireland. Tacitus describes how Agricola planned to lead an expedition there in the company of an Irish chieftain. Juvenal also claims that Roman troops had gone 'beyond the shores of Ireland'. Even native tradition speaks of an exiled Irish prince called Tuathal Techtmar, who returns to claim his kingdom with the help of troops from Britain. Though Roman finds are rare, where they do occur it is in places in the south east of Ireland associated with the Tuathal myth. Whilst the historians were bickering over such matters, archaeologists further complicated things by discovering what has been claimed to be a forty acre Roman fort just fifteen miles north of Dublin at Drumanagh. Coins from the first and second centuries suggest that, if not a conventional Roman fort with a Roman garrison, Drumanagh was at least a substantial native settlement with strong connections to Britain and the distant world of Rome.

Celtic Longsword
1st Century AD
(Perry Collection)

Hittite and Egyptian armies clash at Kadesh.

After the collapse of the Assyrian empire the Egyptians rose up to assert their independence. The 26th or Saite dynasty took control of the north of Egypt from its capital at Sais in the western delta. The Saite Egyptians expanded eastwards but were defeated and thrown back by the Babylonians. Egypt was finally defeated and added to the growing Persian empire in 525 BC. The army list reflects the anarchy that prevailed after the fall of Assyria with numerous foreign and mercenary contingents available to fill out the native Egyptian forces. Otherwise, the army resembles its contemporaries to some extent – namely the Neo-Assyrians and Babylonians. I have given the option to field the chariots as light or heavy, based on either the Assyrian or Libyan model. This is a difference of interpretation so players should really choose one or the other but not both. The reduction in clash value of the chariot is deliberate and reflects a long-standing Egyptian preference for ranged fighting. The Greeks could represent Kyrenean mercenaries, in which case some chariots might also be Kyrenean. This list can also be used to represent the succeeding Late Dynastic period (28th, 29th and 30th Dynasties) by making all hoplites phalanx and giving all Egyptian spearmen long spears. They might also be given the phalanx rule but it is suggested this is reduced to a level of '1' for +1 point per unit. In a later army the chariots might also be Libyan.

Search: The 26th Dynasty, Psamtik I, Battle of Pelusium

Chariots up to 10% and 1+	Up to one in ten of the units in the army can be chariots and the army must include at least 1 unit of chariots regardless of its size.
Cavalry up to 25%	Up to a quarter of the units in the army can be cavalry.
Infantry 50%+	At least a half of the units in the army must be infantry other than skirmishers.
Greek mercenaries may not outnumber Egyptian spearmen	There must be at least as many units of Egyptian spearmen as units of Greek mercenary hoplites.
Divisions 4+ units	Divisions must contain at least 4 units excluding skirmishers and be led by a commander, unless it comprises Greek mercenaries. Greek mercenary hoplites must form their own division regardless of size. A Greek mercenary division may also include Greek javelin-armed skirmishers as noted below. Egyptian Guard spearmen and bowmen must form part of the general's division when present.
Skirmishers per division 50% of infantry	Divisions may contain up to half as many skirmisher units as they contain non-skirmisher infantry.

Saite Egyptian Troop Values

Unit	Combat				Morale Save	Stamina	Special	Points Value
	Clash	Sustained	Short Range	Long Range				
Egyptian medium infantry spearmen	6	6	3	0	5+	6		23 per unit
• *Extra to give Egyptian spearmen long spears*	6	6	3/0	0	5+	6		+3 per unit
• *Reduction to make Egyptian spearmen or long spears levy*	————————— As above —————————						Levy	–3 per unit
• *Extra to make Egyptian spearmen or long spears guard – up to 1 unit*	————————— As above —————————						Elite, Tough fighters	+4 per unit
Egyptian medium infantry bowmen	5	5	3	3	5+	6		24 per unit
• *Reduction to make Egyptian bowmen levy*	5	5	3	3	5+	6	Levy	–3 per unit
• *Extra to make Egyptian bowmen guard – up to 1 unit*	5	5	3	3	5+	6	Elite, Marksmen	+4 per unit
Greek mercenary hoplite heavy infantry with long spears	7	7	3/0	0	4+	6		29 per unit
• *Extra to make Greek hoplites phalanx*	7	7	3/0	0	4+	6	Phalanx	+3 per unit
◦ *Extra to make Greek hoplite phalanx elite*	7	7	3/0	0	4+	6	Phalanx, Elite	+3 per unit
Nubian light infantry with bows	4	4	3	3	0	6		20 per unit
Egyptian, Libyan or Greek skirmishers with javelins fielded as small units	3	2	2	0	0	4		11 per unit
Egyptian or Nubian skirmishers with slings or bows fielded as small units	2	2	2	2	0	4		12 per unit
Scythian horse archers fielded as small units	4	2	2	2	6+	4	Parthian shot	19 per unit
Egyptian or Arab light cavalry with spears and/or javelins	7	5	3	0	6+	6	Feigned flight	28 per unit

Unit	Combat				Morale Save	Stamina	Special	Points Value
	Clash	Sustained	Short Range	Long Range				
Egyptian or Arab light cavalry with spears and/or javelins fielded as small units	5	3	2	0	6+	4		17 per unit
Arab camel-riding light cavalry armed with javelins and bows fielded as small units	5	3	2	2	6+	4	Feigned flight	21 per unit
Egyptian four-horse light chariot with crews armed with bows and javelins	7	6	3	3	4+	6		31 per unit
Egyptian four-horse heavy chariot with crews armed with bows and javelins	8	5	3	3	3+	6		32 per unit
Commanders	1 commander must be provided per division. All commanders including general have leadership 8.							Free

LYDIAN

7th-mid 6th centuries BC

The period covered by this army straddles both the Biblical and Classical ages as we have arbitrarily defined them. The Lydians allied with the Assyrians to fight the fearsome Cimmerian horsemen who descended upon Anatolia from the Pontic Steppes. The powerful Lydian kingdom later went on to defy the might of the Persians under Cyrus the Great, if only briefly. Spear-armed infantry have been treated as pre-hoplite types in the list below. Spearmen could arguably be upgraded to Greek-style heavy infantry in the last decades of Lydian independence in the 6th Century. Chariots fell out of use as the Lydian nobles transformed into an elite mounted arm. I have given stats for both in the lists, treating the Lydian chariots as four-horse light chariots, but an army should really have chariots or Lydian cavalry and not both. Having said that Xenophon, the Greek historian, claims there were Egyptian chariots fighting for the Lydians at the Battle of Thymbra in 547 BC, so there is a precedent! Lydian armies would include lighter troops from the mountainous areas of western Anatolia such as Paphlagonia and Phrygia, as well as levies from the Greek cities of Ionia.

Search: Croesus, Sardis, The Battle of Halys, The Battle of Thymbra.

Infantry 25%+	At least a quarter of the army must be infantry other than skirmishers.
Spearmen 50%+ of infantry	At least half of the non-skirmishing infantry units in the army must be Lydian or mercenary Greek spearmen.
Cavalry 25%+	At least a quarter of the army must be cavalry unless chariots are included in which case there is no obligation.
Chariots up to 10%	Up to one in ten of the units in the army can be chariots so long as no elite cavalry are included.
Divisions 4+ units	Divisions must contain at least 4 units excluding skirmishers and must be led by a commander.
Skirmishers per division 50% of infantry	Divisions may contain up to half as many skirmisher units as they contain non-skirmisher infantry.

Lydian Troop Values								
Unit	Combat				Morale Save	Stamina	Special	Points Value
	Clash	Sustained	Short Range	Long Range				
Lydian spearmen medium infantry armed with spears and/or javelins	6	6	3	0	5+	6		23 per unit
• *Reduction to field Lydian spearmen as levy*	6	6	3	0	5+	6	Levy	–3 per unit
Greek mercenary spearmen armed with long spears	6	6	3/0	0	5+	6		26 per unit
• *Extra to make Greek spearmen phalanx*	6	6	3/0	0	5+	6	Phalanx	+3 per unit
◦ *Extra to make Greek spearmen phalanx elite – up to 1 unit*	7	7	3/0	0	5+	6	Phalanx, Elite	+5 per unit

Lydian Troop Values

Unit	Combat				Morale Save	Stamina	Special	Points Value
	Clash	Sustained	Short Range	Long Range				
Phrygian or Paphlagonian light infantry with spears and/or javelins fielded as small units	3	3	2	0	6+	4		13 per unit
Skirmishers armed with javelins and fielded as small units	3	2	2	0	0	4		11 per unit
• Extra to give skirmishers bows instead of javelins – up to half the skirmisher units	2	2	2	2	0	4		+1 per unit
Lydian medium cavalry armed with spears	8	5	3	0	5+	6	Tough fighters	28 per unit
• Extra to field Lydian cavalry as heavy cavalry elite – up to 1 unit	9	6	3	0	4+	6	Tough fighters, Elite	+6 per unit
Phrygian or Paphlagonian light cavalry armed with javelins and fielded as small units	5	3	2	0	6+	4		17 per unit
Cimmerian horse archers fielded as a small unit – up to 1 unit	4	2	2	2	6+	4	Parthian shot	19 per unit
Four-horse light chariots with crews armed with spears and javelins	8	6	3	0	4+	6		29 per unit
Commanders	1 commander must be provided per division. All commanders including general have leadership 8.							Free

> "Vitellius' ruling vices were extravagance and cruelty. He banqueted three and often four times a day, namely morning, noon, afternoon and evening – the last meal being mainly a drinking bout!"
>
> Suetonius, *The Twelve Caesars* on Vitellius

KYRENEAN GREEK
7th-4th centuries BC

Kyrene on the coast of Africa was colonised by Greeks who founded five cities and promptly fell to fighting amongst themselves as well as with the native Libyans. They were eventually absorbed into Alexander the Great's empire and later that of the Ptolemies. I have based the chariots on the Libyan model as the Kyreneans appear to have adopted these from their neighbours. During a civil war one branch of the Kyrenean leadership allied with the Libyans whom they otherwise mostly fought against – in which case chariots and skirmishers can be Libyan. The Kyreneans were always short of manpower, even when they banded together.

Search: Cyrenaica, The Pentapolis, Cyrene, Apollonia, Arsinoe, Berenice, Barca.

Infantry 75%+	At least three quarters of units in the army must be infantry other than skirmishers.
Hoplites 25-50% of infantry	At least a quarter and no more than half of the non-skirmisher infantry units in the army must be hoplites of one type or another.
Cavalry up to 20%	Up to one in five units in the army can be cavalry.
Chariots up to 10%	Up to one in ten units in the army can be chariots.
Divisions 4+ units unless cavalry and/or chariots	Divisions must contain at least 4 units excluding skirmishers and be led by a commander unless they comprise cavalry and/or chariots only. A division consisting entirely of cavalry and/or chariots can be any size so long as it includes all the cavalry and all the chariots in the army.
Skirmishers per division 50% of infantry	Divisions may contain up to half as many skirmisher units as they contain non-skirmisher infantry.

Unit	Combat				Morale Save	Stamina	Special	Points Value
	Clash	Sustained	Short Range	Long Range				

Kyrenean Greek Troop Values

Unit	Clash	Sustained	Short Range	Long Range	Morale Save	Stamina	Special	Points Value
Heavy infantry hoplites armed with long spears	7	7	3/0	0	4+	6		29 per unit
• *Extra to make Greek hoplites phalanx*	7	7	3/0	0	4+	6	*Phalanx*	+3 per unit
◦ *Extra to make Greek hoplite phalanx elite*	7	7	3/0	0	4+	6	*Phalanx, Elite*	+3 per unit
Light infantry peltasts with spears/javelins	5	5	3	0	6+	6		20 per unit
• *Reduction to field light infantry peltasts as small units*	3	3	2	0	6+	4		−7 per unit
Skirmishers armed with javelins and fielded as small units	3	2	2	0	0	4		11 per unit
• *Extra to give skirmishers slings or bows instead of javelins – up to half the skirmisher units*	2	2	2	2	0	4		+1 per unit
Medium cavalry fielded as a small units	6	3	2	0	5+	4		19 per unit
Light cavalry armed with javelins and fielded as a small units	5	3	2	0	6+	4		17 per unit
Kyrenean four-horse light chariots with javelin-armed crews	8	6	3	0	4+	6		29 per unit
Commanders			1 commander must be provided per division. All commanders including general have leadership 8.					Free

EARLY ACHAEMENID PERSIAN

6th-5th centuries BC

This is the classic Persian army of the time of the wars against Greece and as such will be familiar to many with an interest in ancient history and warfare. It is a multi-ethnic army – as described at some length by the ancient historian Herodotus – with a core of Medes and Persians. The Achaemenid Empire stretched from Greece to India and included Egypt in the south and the coast of the Black Sea in the North, making it one of the largest empires of the ancient Near East. The army affords a good mix of cavalry and infantry; the infantry combine ranged shooting and hand-to-hand combat in the usual fashion for many Near Eastern armies. The Persian sparabara refers to the 'spara' shield – a tall, oblong shield carried by the front ranks of mixed formations and often used to form an improvised barrier. This is represented by allowing the –1 to hit by ranged fire from the front in the same way as for formations of heavy infantry. No point cost has been allocated for this. Although I've only included the note as part of the sparabara, the rule can be extended to other units where they have the same large spara shield, if players wish.

Search: Cyrus the Great, The Battle of Pteria, Cambyses II, The Battle of Pelusium, Darius the Great, Xerxes, The Greco-Persian Wars.

Cavalry up to 50%	Up to half the units in the army can be cavalry.
Infantry 25%+	At least a quarter of the units in the army must be infantry other than skirmishers.
Sparabara 25%+ of infantry	At least a quarter of the non-skirmisher infantry units in the army must be sparabara.
Levy 25%+ of infantry	At least a quarter of non-skirmisher infantry units in the army must be levy.
Mercenary hoplites up to 25% of infantry	Up to a quarter of the non-skirmisher infantry units in the army can be hoplites.
Heavy scythed chariots up to 3 units	Up to three units in the army can be heavy scythed chariots.
Divisions 4+ units	Divisions must contain at least 4 units excluding skirmishers and be led by a commander. Hoplites must be organized into hoplite divisions consisting entirely of hoplites, or hoplites and javelin-armed skirmisher units as noted below.
Skirmishers per division 50% of infantry	Divisions may contain up to half as many skirmisher units as they contain non-skirmisher infantry.

Early Achaemenid Persian Troop Values

Unit	Clash	Sustained	Short Range	Long Range	Morale Save	Stamina	Special	Points Value
		Combat						
Immortal medium infantry with spears and bows	6	6	3	3	5+	6	Stubborn, Marksmen	29 per unit
Iranian/Mede sparabara medium infantry with mixed spears and bows.	6	6	3	3	5+	6	Sparabara (See notes)	26 per unit
Medium infantry levy with spears	6	6	3	0	5+	6	Levy	20 per unit
Medium infantry levy armed with bows	5	5	3	3	5+	6	Levy	21 per unit
Heavy infantry mercenary hoplites armed with long spears	7	7	3/0	0	4+	6	Elite, Phalanx	35 per unit
Skirmishers with javelins fielded as small units	3	2	2	0	0	4		11 per unit
• *Extra to give skirmishers slings instead of javelins – up to half the skirmisher units*	2	2	2	2	0	4		+1 per unit
• *Extra to give skirmishers bows instead of javelins – up to half the skirmisher units*	2	2	2	2	0	4		+1 per unit
• *Reduction to field any skirmisher units as levy*	————— As above —————						Levy	-2 per unit
Light cavalry armed with javelins fielded as small units	5	3	2	0	6+	4	Feigned flight	19 per unit
• *Extra to replace light cavalry javelins with bows – up to half*	5	3	2	2	6+	4	Feigned flight	+2 per unit
• *Reduction to field any light cavalry units as levy*	————— As above —————						Feigned flight, Levy	–2 per unit
Horse archers fielded as small units	4	2	2	2	6+	4	Parthian shot	19 per unit
Heavy cavalry guard with spears and bows – up to 1 unit	9	6	3	2	4+	6	Stubborn, Marksmen	36 per unit
Medium cavalry armed with spears and bows	8	5	3	2	5+	6		29 per unit
• *Reduction to field medium cavalry without bows – up to 1 unit*	8	5	3	0	5+	6		–2 per unit
• *Extra to upgrade medium cavalry with spears and bows to heavy cavalry – up to half*	9	6	3	2	4+	6		+3 per unit
• *Reduction to make heavy or medium cavalry levy – up to half*	————— As above —————						Levy	–3 per unit
Heavy scythed chariot fielded as a unit of 1 model	7	0	0	0	3+	4	Scythed chariot	10 per unit
Arab camel-mounted light cavalry with bows and javelins fielded as a small unit – up to 1 unit	4	3	2	2	6+	4	Feigned flight	20 per unit
Commanders	1 commander must be provided per division. All commanders including general have leadership 8.							Free
• *Upgrade hoplite commanders*	*Any commanders of hoplite divisions can be upgraded to leadership 9.*							25 each

EARLY CARTHAGINIAN   6th-3rd centuries BC

This army represents the forces of Carthage during the expansion of her domains in Africa and the first conflicts with Greek colonies in the western Mediterranean. This is a period during the history of Carthage that is less well-documented or understood than the later period of wars against Rome. However, it is during these years that the power of Carthage was at its greatest extent. It is therefore an interesting subject for a wargames army even if it must be, to some extent, a speculative one. It is a multi-ethnic army that contains various mercenaries as well as local North African troops. Greek mercenary hoplites were also employed, specifically after the Carthaginians' poor showing at the Battle of the Krimisos in 341 BC, and could be included in an army of this period (see the Hoplite Greek list for stats). Carthaginian cavalry are given reduced attacks on the basis they were poorer even than Greeks. I have chosen to represent chariots as light chariots, making them mobile fighting platforms rather than lumbering wagons, albeit pulled by four horses. This is, of course, arguable, and those wishing to employ heavy chariots are welcome to make the change. Skirmishers can be any of the nations represented and would typically be Numidians or Libyans.

Search: Tyre, Queen Dido, The Magonids, Hanno, Himilco, the Greek-Punic Wars, The Battle of Himera.

Infantry 50%+	At least half of units in the army must be infantry other than skirmishers.
Cavalry up to 25%	Up to a quarter of the units in the army can be cavalry.
Light Cavalry 50%+ of cavalry	At least half of the cavalry units in the army must be light cavalry.
Chariots up to 25%	Up to a quarter of the units in the army can be chariots.
Divisions 4+ units	Divisions must contain at least 4 units other than skirmishers and be led by a commander. Libyan warbands and chariots can only be included as part of allied divisions consisting entirely of Libyans. Libyan divisions can include Libyan skirmishers as noted below.
Skirmishers per division 50% of infantry	Divisions may contain up to half as many skirmisher units as they contain non-skirmisher infantry.

Early Carthaginian Troop Values

Unit	Combat				Morale Save	Stamina	Special	Points Value
	Clash	Sustained	Short Range	Long Range				
African medium infantry with long spears	6	6	3/0	0	5+	6		26 per unit
• Extra to make African medium infantry phalanx	6	6	3/0	0	5+	6	Phalanx	+3 per unit
Carthaginian heavy infantry with long spears	7	7	3/0	0	4+	6		29 per unit
• Extra to make heavy infantry phalanx	7	7	3/0	0	4+	6	Phalanx	+3 per unit
Sacred Band heavy infantry with long spears – up to 1 unit	7	7	3/0	0	4+	6	Elite, Tough fighters	33 per unit
• Extra to make Sacred Band phalanx	7	7	3/0	0	4+	6	Elite, Tough fighters, Phalanx	+3 per unit
Gallic medium infantry warband armed with swords and javelins	9	6	2	0	5+	6	Wild fighters	28 per unit
Spanish scutarii light infantry armed with pila	5	5	3	0	6+	6		23 per unit
Ligurian light infantry armed with double-handed axes	6	5	2/0	0	6+	6		21 per unit
Ligurian, Sardinian or Corsican light infantry armed with javelins	5	5	3	0	6+	6		20 per unit
Libyan light infantry warband with javelins	7	5	2	0	6+	6		21 per unit
Skirmishers armed with javelins and fielded as small units	3	2	2	0	0	4		11 per unit
Spanish Balearic skirmishers with slings	2	2	2	2	0	4	Marksmen	13 per unit
Ligurian skirmishers with slings – up to 1 unit	2	2	2	2	0	4		12 per unit
Sardinian skirmishers with bows– up to 1 unit	2	2	2	2	0	4		12 per unit
Carthaginian medium cavalry fielded as a small unit – up to 1 unit	5	3	2	0	5+	4		18 per unit
Greek, Etruscan or Campanian medium cavalry fielded as small units	6	3	2	0	5+	4		19 per unit
Numidian light cavalry armed with javelins and fielded as small units	5	3	2	0	6+	4	Feigned flight	19 per unit
Medium artillery bolt throwers	1	1	0	3	0	3		20 per unit
Carthaginian or Libyan four-horse light chariots with javelin-armed crews	8	6	3	0	4+	6		29 per unit
Commanders	1 commander must be provided per division. All commanders including general have leadership 8.							Free
• Upgrade hoplite commanders	Any commanders of hoplite divisions can be upgraded to leadership 9.							25 each

This list represents the Greek armies from the time of the wars against Persia. This army has a heavy emphasis on hoplites and very little room for skirmishers and cavalry as seems appropriate for these early Greeks. More light troops and cavalry were included in later years, and it is left to players to relax the restrictions accordingly where they feel it appropriate to do so. Hoplites of the immediately preceding period often carried a second spear to throw, and I've taken it as read that this practice had been discontinued by the time of the Persian wars. Should players wish, this dual-arming can be represented by restoring a full 'short range' value of 3 to hoplite units rather than the split value of 3/0. One unit of light cavalry and one small unit of light infantry peltasts can form a combined hamippoi unit with both treated as sub-units of the other. Hamippoi were trained to fight alongside horsemen and keep up with them. So long as hamippoi infantry remain within 6" of their cavalry whilst both move their move rate is increased to 9". Hamippoi count as cavalry for the purposes of forming a 'cavalry only' division.

Search: The Ionian Revolt, The Battle of Marathon, The Battle of Thermopylae, The Battle of Plataea.

Infantry 75%+	At least three quarters of the units in the army must be infantry other than skirmishers.
Hoplites 75%+ of infantry	At least three quarters of the non-skirmisher infantry units in the army must comprise hoplites of one kind or another.
Spartans up to 50% of hoplites	Up to half of hoplite units can be Spartans.
Cavalry up to 10%	Up to one in ten of the units in the army can be cavalry.
Divisions 4+ units unless cavalry	Divisions must contain at least 4 units unless they comprise cavalry only. A division consisting entirely of cavalry can be any size so long as it includes all the cavalry in the army. Each division must be led by a commander.
Skirmishers per division 25% of infantry	Divisions may contain up to a quarter as many skirmisher units as they contain non-skirmisher infantry.

Hoplite Greek Troop Values

Unit	Clash	Sustained	Short Range	Long Range	Morale Save	Stamina	Special	Points Value
Spartan heavy infantry hoplites armed with long spears	7	7	3/0	0	4+	6	Drilled, Stubborn, Elite, Phalanx	41 per unit
Elite hoplite heavy infantry armed with long spears	7	7	3/0	0	4+	6	Elite, Phalanx	35 per unit
Hoplite heavy infantry armed with long spears	7	7	3/0	0	4+	6	Phalanx	32 per unit
Levy hoplite heavy infantry armed with long spears	6	6	3/0	0	4+	6	Levy, Phalanx	27 per unit
Light infantry peltasts with spears/javelins	5	5	3	0	6+	6		20 per unit
• *Reduction to field light infantry peltasts as small units*	3	3	2	0	6+	4		–7 per unit
Skirmishers armed with javelins and fielded as small units	3	2	2	0	0	4		11 per unit
• *Extra to give skirmishers slings instead of javelins – up to half the skirmisher units*	2	2	2	2	0	4		+1 per unit
° *Extra to upgrade skirmisher slingers to Rhodians – up to 1 unit*	2	2	2	2	0	4	Marksmen	+1 per unit
• *Extra to give skirmishers bows instead of javelins – up to 1 unit*	2	2	2	2	0	4		+1 per unit
° *Extra to upgrade skirmisher bowmen to Cretans*	2	2	2	2	0	4	Marksmen	+1 per unit
Medium cavalry fielded as small units	6	3	2	0	5+	4		19 per unit
Light cavalry armed with javelins and fielded as small units	5	3	2	0	6+	4		17 per unit
• *Extra to upgrade light cavalry Thessalians – up to 1 unit*	5	3	2	0	6+	4	Feigned Flight	+2 per unit
Commanders		1 commander must be provided per division. All commanders including general have leadership 8.						Free
• *Extra to upgrade general to leadership 9*		*If the army includes its maximum quota of Spartan hoplites a Spartan general can lead it. A Spartan general has leadership 9 and can add up to a maximum of 6 attacks in hand-to-hand combat rather than the usual 3.*						+25

Thrace was the name given by the Greeks to the lands to their north inhabited by barbarians that they called Thracians. In Greek usage the term was therefore somewhat imprecise, but by Thrace we generally refer to the eastern Balkans. The Thracians were closely related to the Bithynians east of the Hellespont and the Dacians to the North (modern Romania). Part of Thrace was absorbed into the Empire of Alexander the Great and his successors and Thracians fought as mercenaries in Hellenistic armies. The classic Thracian troop type is the peltast armed with a mix of long and light spears and often carrying the characteristic rhomphaia, a heavy scythe-like weapon that is probably comparable to the Dacian falx. In our list Thracian peltasts with mixed long spears and javelins count the long spear rule but retain a short ranged attack. Peltasts cannot carry both long spears and rhomphaia. The Thracians hired out to surrounding Greek and Hellenistic states, and likewise Thracian armies could include Greek hoplites as mercenaries – see the Greek Hoplite and Later Hoplite Greek lists for suitable stats.

Search: The Getae, The Odrysian Kingdom, King Cotys, Seuthopolis, Paeonians.

Cavalry up to 25%	Up to a quarter of the units in the army can be cavalry.
Infantry 75%+	At least three quarters of the units in the army must be infantry other than skirmishers.
Peltasts 50%+ of infantry	At least half the non-skirmisher infantry in the army must be peltasts.
Divisions 4+ units	Divisions must contain at least 4 units and be led by a commander.
Skirmishers per division 50% of infantry	Divisions may contain up to half as many skirmisher units as they contain non-skirmisher infantry.

Thracian Troop Values

Unit	Clash	Sustained	Short Range	Long Range	Morale Save	Stamina	Special	Points Value
Medium cavalry with javelins – up to 1 unit	8	5	3	0	5+	6		27 per unit
Light cavalry armed with javelins and fielded as small units	5	3	2	0	6+	4		17 per unit
Peltast light infantry armed with javelins and shields	5	5	3	0	6+	6		20 per unit
• Extra to field peltasts as mixed javelins and long spear	5	5	3	0	6+	6		+3 per unit
○ Extra to make long spear peltasts tough fighters	5	5	3	0	6+	6	Tough fighters	+1 per unit
• Extra to give peltasts double-handed rhomphaia and javelins	6	5	3	0	6+	6		+2 per unit
○ Extra to make rhomphaia peltasts tough fighters	6	5	3	0	6+	6	Tough fighters	+1 per unit
Light infantry archers – up to 1 unit	4	4	3	3	0	6		20 per unit
• Reduction to field light infantry archers as small units	3	3	2	2	0	4		–6 per unit
Skirmishers with javelins fielded as small units	3	2	2	0	0	4		11 per unit
Skirmishers with slings fielded as a small unit – up to 1 unit	2	2	2	2	0	4		12 per unit
Commanders		1 commander must be provided per division. All commanders including general have Leadership 8.						Free

Greek hoplites arrayed for battle.

The term Samnite was used by the Romans to describe the inhabitants of Samnium, a region of central and southern Italy. They fought a series of wars against the Romans in the 4th and early 3rd centuries BC, and allied with Hannibal against the Romans during the Second Punic War. They often fought in concert with other Italians against Rome and the list reflects the support of Oscan, Campanian and other allies. In later times the Samnites revolted against the Romans in the Social War of 91-88 BC.

Search: The Samnite Wars, The Caudine Forks, The Battle of Aquilonia, The Linen Legion.

Cavalry up to 25%	Up to a quarter of the units in the army can be cavalry.
Samnite/Lucanian light cavalry 50%+ of cavalry	At least half the cavalry units in the army must be Samnite or Lucanian light cavalry.
Infantry 75%+	At least three quarters of the units in the army must be infantry other than skirmishers.
Samnite light infantry 25%+ of infantry	At least a quarter of the non-skirmisher infantry units in the army must be Samnite light infantry.
Divisions 4+ units	Divisions must contain at least 4 units excluding skirmishers and be led by a commander.
Skirmishers per division 25% of infantry	Divisions may contain up to a quarter as many skirmisher units as they contain non-skirmisher infantry.

Samnite Troop Values

Unit	Combat				Morale Save	Stamina	Special	Points Value
	Clash	Sustained	Short Range	Long Range				
Samnite medium infantry armed with spears	6	6	3	0	5+	6		23 per unit
• *Extra to give Samnite infantry pila – up to half*	6	6	3	0	5+	6		+3 *per unit*
Samnite Linen Legion medium infantry	6	6	3	0	5+	6	Stubborn	25 per unit
• *Extra to give medium Linen Legion pila*	6	6	3	0	5+	6	Stubborn	+3 *per unit*
Samnite Linen Legion heavy infantry	7	7	3	0	4+	6	Stubborn	29 per unit
• *Extra to give heavy Linen Legion pila*	7	7	3	0	4+	6	Stubborn	+3 *per unit*
Oscan medium infantry with pila	6	6	3	0	5+	6		26 per unit
Oscan or Campanian heavy infantry hoplites with long spears – up to 1 unit	7	7	3/0	0	4+	6	Phalanx	32 per unit
Lucanian heavy infantry with long spears fielded as a small unit – up to 1 unit	5	5	2/0	0	4+	4	Phalanx	23 per unit
Samnite light infantry armed with javelins	5	5	3	0	6+	6		20 per unit
• *Extra to make Samnite light infantry drilled*	5	5	3	0	6+	6	Drilled	+3 *per unit*
• *Extra to make Samnite light infantry elite*	5	5	3	0	6+	6	Drilled, Elite	+6 *per unit*
• *Extra to make any of the above tough fighters*	5	5	3	0	6+	6	As above + Tough fighters	+1 *per unit*
Skirmishers armed with javelins and fielded as small units	3	2	2	0	0	4		11 per unit
Peasant skirmishers armed with bows and fielded as a small unit – up to 1 unit	2	2	2	2	0	4	Levy	10 per unit
Peasant skirmishers armed with slings and fielded as a small unit – up to 1 unit	2	2	2	2	0	4	Levy	10 per unit
Samnite or Lucanian light cavalry armed with javelins and fielded as small units	5	3	2	0	6+	4	Feigned flight	19 per unit
Tarentine or Apulian light cavalry armed with javelins and fielded as small units	5	3	2	0	6+	4	Elite	19 per unit
• *Extra to make Tarentine cavalry stubborn*	5	3	2	0	6+	4	Elite, Stubborn	+1 *per unit*
Campanian light cavalry armed with javelins and fielded as a small unit – up to 1 unit	5	3	2	0	6+	4	Elite, Feigned flight	21 per unit
Apulian medium cavalry with spears fielded as a small unit – up to 1 unit	6	3	2	0	5+	4		19 per unit
Commanders	1 commander must be provided per division. All commanders including general have leadership 8.							Free

This army list represents the Greek forces of the Peloponnesian War which broke out in 460 BC, although the term is usually reserved for the war between Athens and Sparta lasting from 431-404 BC. It also covers the Greek armies down to the Macedonian conquest and immediately afterwards. This army has obvious parallels with the early Greeks and has a similar, though slightly reduced, emphasis on the hoplite. I have allowed for more skirmishers and a greater proportion of light troops overall. I have drawn up a broad-based list and leave it to players to include Spartans only in armies fighting for Sparta – though Theban Sacred Band might be accorded the same status. One unit of light cavalry and one small unit of light infantry peltasts can form a combined hamippoi unit with both treated as sub-units of the other. Hamippoi were trained to fight alongside horsemen and keep up with them. So long as hamippoi infantry remain within 6" of their cavalry whilst both move their move rate is increased to 9".

Search: The Delian League, The Peloponnesian War, The Battle of Mantinea, The Sicilian Expedition, The Corinthian War, The Battle of Leuctra, The Third Sacred War.

Infantry 75%+	At least three quarters of units in the army must be infantry other than skirmishers.
Hoplites 50%+ of infantry	At least half of the non-skirmisher infantry units in the army must be hoplites of one kind or another.
Spartans up to 50% of hoplites	Up to half of hoplite units can be Spartans.
Cavalry up to 25%	Up to a quarter of the units in the army can be cavalry.
Divisions 4+ units	Divisions must contain at least 4 units excluding skirmishers and must be led by a commander.
Skirmishers per division 50% of infantry	Divisions may contain up to half as many skirmisher units as they contain non-skirmisher infantry.

Later Hoplite Greek Troop Values

Unit	Clash	Sustained	Short Range	Long Range	Morale Save	Stamina	Special	Points Value
Spartan heavy infantry hoplites armed with long spears	7	7	3/0	0	4+	6	Drilled, Stubborn, Elite, Phalanx	41 per unit
Elite hoplite heavy infantry armed with long spears	7	7	3/0	0	4+	6	Elite, Phalanx	35 per unit
Hoplite heavy infantry armed with long spears	7	7	3/0	0	4+	6	Phalanx	32 per unit
Levy hoplites heavy infantry armed with long spears	6	6	3/0	0	4+	6	Levy, Phalanx	27 per unit
Thorakitai heavy infantry with spears and javelins	7	7	3	0	4+	6		26 per unit
Thureophoroi medium infantry with spears and javelins	6	6	3	0	5+	6		23 per unit
Light infantry peltasts with spears/javelins	5	5	3	0	6+	6		20 per unit
• *Reduction to field light infantry peltasts as small units*	3	3	2	0	6+	4		*–7 per unit*
Skirmishers armed with javelins and fielded as small units	3	2	2	0	0	4		11 per unit
• *Extra to give skirmishers slings instead of javelins – up to half the skirmisher units*	2	2	2	2	0	4		*+1 per unit*
○ *Extra to upgrade skirmisher slingers to Rhodians – up to 1 unit*	2	2	2	2	0	4	Marksmen	*+1 per unit*
• *Extra to give skirmishers bows instead of javelins – up to 1 unit*	2	2	2	2	0	4		*+1 per unit*
○ *Extra to upgrade skirmisher bowmen to Cretans*	2	2	2	2	0	4	Marksmen	*+1 per unit*
Medium cavalry fielded as small units	6	3	2	0	5+	4		19 per unit
Light cavalry armed with javelins and fielded as small units	5	3	2	0	6+	4		17 per unit
• *Extra to upgrade light cavalry to Thessalians – up to 1 unit*	5	3	2	0	6+	4	Feigned flight	*+2 per unit*
Commanders	1 commander must be provided per division. All commanders including general have leadership 8.							Free
• *Extra to upgrade general to leadership 9*	*If the army includes its maximum quota of Spartan hoplites a Spartan general can lead it. A Spartan general has leadership 9 and can add up to 6 attacks in hand-to-hand combat instead of the usual 3.*							*+25*

This list describes the armies that confronted Alexander the Great as well as his successors in the East. In the wake of Alexander's death Chandragupta Maurya rose to become the first ruler of a unified India. The dynasty he founded lasted until the early 2nd century BC. According to the ancient historian Arrian, Indian society was divided into castes that included hereditary warriors, and he goes on to describe types of chariots and much about the fighting methods of the Indians. I have chosen to arrange the Indian archer and spear-armed troops into mixed units as this seems inherently likely and seems to fit the general character and fighting method of the army. Indian cavalry performed poorly against the Macedonians and seem to have been of lowly status compared to the chariots and elephants. I have described the fighting cavalry as medium but reduced their clash value to that of light troops – without the advantage of being able to fight in open order. Chariots could be very large with numerous draught animals that could include teams of oxen! The largest would have four wheels akin to wagons – it seems unlikely such lumbering hulks would have much impact in combat. Indian states with few elephants would use large, heavy wagon-like chariots to try and compensate for their lack, and these would be stuffed with archers. I have represented these with the ox-drawn heavy chariots, reducing their clash vaue appropriately. Ox-drawn chariots/wagons are limited to a single move each turn regardless of how successfully an order is issued. It is certainly a colourful army and one that features both elephants and chariots in considerable amounts! Cavalry were not considered especially prestigious amongst the Indians, who reserved chariots and elephants for the true elites – commanders would be likely to ride one or the other.

Search: King Poros, Battle of the Hydaspes, Chandragupta Maurya, Maurya Empire, Ashoka the Great, the Seleucid-Mauryan War, Megasthenes, Arrian's Indica

Infantry 50%+	At least a half of the units in the army must be infantry other than skirmishers.
Warrior caste 50%+ of infantry	At least half the non-skirmisher infantry units in the army must be warrior caste troops of one kind or another.
Cavalry up to 25%	Up to a quarter of the units in the army can be cavalry.
Chariots up to 25%	Up to a quarter of the units in the army can be chariots.
Elephants up to 20%	Up to one in five of the units in the army can be elephants.
Artillery up to 2	Up to one unit of each type can be included and no more than one in ten of the number of units in the army in total.
Divisions 4+ units	Divisions must contain at least 4 units excluding skirmishers, unless consisting of mercenaries in which case they can be smaller as noted below. Chariots, cavalry and elephants cannot be mixed in the same division. Mercenaries must form a single division of 1 or more units unless there are more than 5 units in total excluding skirmishers, in which case they can be organised into two separate divisions for ease of command. All divisions must have a commander.
Skirmishers per division 50% of infantry or 1 per elephant	Divisions may contain up to half as many skirmisher units as they contain non-skirmisher infantry. Elephants can have skirmishers as sub-units as noted.

Pauravan and Mauryan Indians Troop Values

Unit	Combat				Morale Save	Stamina	Special	Points Value
	Clash	Sustained	Short Range	Long Range				
Heavy infantry guards armed with spears and javelins– up to 1 unit	7	7	3	0	4+	6	Tough fighters	27 per unit
• *Extra to give guards double-handed swords – up to 1 unit*	8	7	2/0	0	4+	6	*Tough fighters*	*+1 per unit*
Warrior caste medium infantry with mixed ranks of spears/javelins and bows	6	6	3	3	5+	6		26 per unit
Warrior caste medium infantry armed with bows	5	5	3	3	5+	6		24 per unit
Guildsmen levy medium infantry with bows	5	5	3	3	5+	6	Levy	21 per unit
Mercenary medium infantry with spears and javelins	6	6	3	3	5+	6	Stubborn	28 per unit
Mercenary medium infantry with bows	5	5	3	3	5+	6	Marksmen	25 per unit

Unit	Combat				Morale Save	Stamina	Special	Points Value
	Clash	Sustained	Short Range	Long Range				
Skirmishers armed with javelins and fielded as small units	3	2	2	0	0	4		11 per unit
• Extra to give skirmishers slings instead of javelins – up to 1 unit	2	2	2	2	0	4		+1 per unit
• Extra to give skirmishers bows instead of javelins – up to 1 unit	2	2	2	2	0	4		+1 per unit
Medium cavalry armed with spears/javelins	7	5	3	0	5+	6		26 per unit
Light cavalry armed with javelins and fielded as small units	5	3	2	0	6+	4		17 per unit
Light chariots with spear/javelin-armed crews	6	6	3	0	4+	6		27 per unit
• Extra to equip light chariots with bow armed crews	6	6	3	3	4+	6		+3 per unit
Heavy chariots with spear/javelin-armed crews	9	5	3	0	3+	6		30 per unit
• Extra to equip heavy chariots with bow armed crew	9	5	3	3	3+	6		+3 per unit
• Extra to make any chariot unit elite regardless of armament	———————— As above ————————						Elite	+3 per unit
Ox-drawn heavy chariot 'anti-elephant wagon' with bow-armed crews	5	5	3	3	3+	6	See notes	29 per unit
Elephant with crew armed with spears, javelins and bows	4	3	1	1	4+	6	Elephant	24 per unit
Sub-unit of skirmishers fielded as small units – up to 1 per elephant	3	2	2	0	0	4		11 per unit
Light artillery – up to 1 unit	1	1	2	2	0	3		15 per unit
Medium artillery – up to 1 unit	1	1	0	3	0	3		20 per unit
Commanders	1 commander must be provided per division. All commanders including general have leadership 8							Free

SYRACUSAN

4th–early 3rd centuries BC

Syracuse was a Greek colony in Sicily and one of the most powerful and influential cities of the western Mediterranean. Although isolated from the principal cities of Greece it played a major part during the Peloponnesian War where its large and powerful navy proved decisive. The Syracusans made the mistake of allying themselves with Carthage against Rome, an error of judgement that led to their annexation by the Romans in 212 BC. This is a varied army with many colourful troop types and I have somewhat emphasised the potential differences to reflect this. Etruscans carrying both long spear and pila can count as either during any turn but never both. As the rules for both weapons only apply during the initial turn of combat this has been costed at 3 points rather than 6.

Search: Dionysius I of Syracuse, Hiero II of Syracuse, Tyrants of Syracuse.

Cavalry up to 33%	Up to a third of the units in the army can be cavalry.
Infantry 50%+	At least half of the units in the army must be infantry other than skirmishers.
Hoplites 25%+ of infantry	At least a quarter of the non-skirmisher infantry units in the army must be hoplites.
Mercenary Hoplites up to 50% of Hoplites	Up to half the hoplite units in the army can be mercenary hoplites including bodyguard.
Artillery up to 3	The army can include up to 3 units of artillery, of which no more than 1 unit can be medium artillery.
Divisions 4+ units	Divisions must contain at least 4 units excluding skirmishers and must be led by a commander.
Skirmishers per division 50% of infantry	Divisions may contain up to half as many skirmisher units as they contain non-skirmisher infantry.

Unit	Combat				Morale Save	Stamina	Special	Points Value
	Clash	Sustained	Short Range	Long Range				
Mercenary hoplite guard heavy infantry armed with long spears – up to 1 unit	7	7	3/0	0	4+	6	Elite, Phalanx	35 per unit
Mercenary hoplite heavy infantry armed with long spears	7	7	3/0	0	4+	6	Phalanx	32 per unit
Syracusan and allied hoplite heavy infantry armed with long spears	6	6	3/0	0	4+	6	Levy, Phalanx	27 per unit
Etruscan heavy infantry armed with mix of long spears and pila – up to 1 unit	7	7	3	0	4+	6	See note	29 per unit
Campanian or Samnite light infantry with spears and javelins	5	5	3	0	6+	6		20 per unit
• Reduction to field light infantry as small units	3	3	2	0	6+	4		-7 per unit
Gallic medium infantry warband with swords and javelins – up to 1 unit	9	6	2	0	5+	6	Wild fighters	28 per unit
Spanish scutarii medium infantry with heavy javelins counting as pila – up to 1 unit	6	6	3	0	5+	6		26 per unit
Skirmishers armed with javelins and fielded as small units	3	2	2	0	0	4		11 per unit
• Extra to give skirmishers slings instead of javelins – up to half the skirmisher units	2	2	2	2	0	4		+1 per unit
• Extra to give skirmishers bows instead of javelins – up to 1 unit	2	2	2	2	0	4		+1 per unit
Greek medium cavalry armed with spears and/or javelins	8	5	3	0	5+	6		27 per unit
Light cavalry armed with javelins and fielded as small units	5	3	2	0	6+	4		17 per unit
Gastraphetes-armed troops counting as light artillery	1	1	2	2	0	3		15 per unit
Bolt-thowing ballista, medium artillery – up to 1 unit	1	1	0	3	0	3		20 per unit
Commanders			1 commander must be provided per division. All commanders including general have leadership 8.					Free

THE DOG OF MARATHON

Following the Greek victory against the Persians at Marathon in 490BC, the Athenians created a painted mural to commemorate the battle. This stood in the northern porch of the market-square – the Agora – alongside murals depicting, amongst other things, Theseus' victory over the Amazons and the sack of Troy. According to the Roman writer Claudius Aelianus – better known as Aelian – the painted scene included a depiction of one of the famous legends surrounding the battle: the tale of the dog of Marathon. This faithful dog is supposed to have followed its master to the Greek camp and to have fought at his side against the Persians.

The story is referred to in Aelian's *On the Nature of Animals*, a work full of all kinds of bizarre stories about animals, some of which later found their way into medieval bestiaries. The murals survived for hundreds of years until removed during the late fourth century by the Roman governor, after which they disappeared.

Bronze 'Luristan' sword
Iran c. 900 BC (Perry Collection)

This is the army of Marcus Furius Camillus and his successors. Camillus was a Roman dictator who fought against the Etruscans and defeated an invading army of Gauls. The classic division of the army into hastati, principes and triarii and their method of fighting is ascribed to Camillus by Livy and has been used as the basis for this list. Note that hastati/principes/triarii can be Romans or Latin allies. The classic Roman three-line fighting formation with hastati at the front, principes behind, and triarii at the rear is difficult to impose upon players who often want to lead with their 'best' troops – namely the triarii. To encourage players to use tactics comparable to our forebears we rule that the loss of hastati units doesn't count for purposes of the division becoming broken. It therefore makes sense to use them for the initial fighting. Triarii, on the other hand, have a close range attack value of 3 for supporting – a bonused value for a small unit – and are therefore ideally placed behind a fighting unit. Representing the smaller Roman tactical formations as small units is visually appealing and seems to feel right. If players prefer to field units at standard size they can certainly do so and suitable stats for full-size units can be extracted from the Marian list. During the Latin War the Romans allied with the Samnites. Stats for Samnite troops can be found in the Samnite list.

Search: The Latin War, The Battle of Vesuvius, The Samnite War, The Battle of Trifanum, The Battle of Allia, Marcus Furius Camillus.

Infantry 75%+	At least three quarters of units in the army must be infantry other than skirmishers. Of these at least half must be hastati, principes and/or triarii as noted below.
Hastati, principes and triarii 50%+ of infantry	Together hastati, principes and triarii must make up at least half the units of non-skirmisher infantry in the army. Hastati and principes units must be bought in pairs – 1 hastati and 1 principes. Triarii can be included in the ratio of up to 1 unit of triarii for every two pairs of hastati/principes, ie, 2 hastati: 2 principes: 1 triarii.
Cavalry up to 20%	Up to one in five of the units in the army can be cavalry.
Divisions 4 units	Divisions must contain at least 4 units excluding skirmishers and must be led by a commander. Allied infantry must be fielded in divisions wholly composed of native troops – this may include leves skirmishers as noted below.
Skirmishers per division 25% of infantry	Divisions may contain up to a quarter as many skirmisher units as they contain non-skirmisher infantry.

Camillan Roman Troop Values

Unit	Clash	Sustained	Short Range	Long Range	Morale Save	Stamina	Special	Points Value
Hastati medium infantry armed with long spears and fielded as small units	4	4	2/0	0	5+	4	Drilled	20 per unit
• *Extra to make hastati heavy infantry*	5	5	2/0	0	4+	4	*Drilled*	*+3 per unit*
◦ *Extra to give hastati heavy infantry pila instead of long spears*	5	5	2	0	4+	4	*Drilled*	*Free*
Principes medium infantry armed with long spears and fielded as small units	4	4	2/0	0	5+	4	Drilled	20 per unit
• *Extra to make principes heavy infantry*	5	5	2/0	0	4+	4	*Drilled*	*+3 per unit*
Triarii heavy infantry armed with long spears and fielded as small units	5	5	3/0	0	4+	4	Drilled, Elite, Stubborn	28 per unit
• *Extra to make triarii valiant*	5	5	3/0	0	4+	4	*Drilled, Elite, Stubborn, Valiant*	*+2 per unit*
Allied Italian medium infantry armed with spears or javelins	6	6	3	0	5+	6		23 per unit
• *Reduction to make allied Italians rorarii levy*	6	6	3	0	5+	6	*Levy*	*–3 per unit*
Leves skirmishers armed with javelins and fielded as small units	3	2	2	0	0	4		11 per unit
Roman or Italian medium cavalry fielded as small units	6	3	2	0	5+	4		19 per unit
• *Extra to upgrade Roman medium cavalry to elite 'Knights of the City' – up to 1 unit*	6	3	2	0	5+	4	*Elite*	*+2 per unit*
Light cavalry armed with javelins and fielded as small units	5	3	2	0	6+	4		17 per unit
Commanders		1 commander must be provided per division. All commanders including general have leadership 8.						Free

The Gauls lived in what is today France and northern Italy. They were skilled metal-workers, and are said to have invented mail armour which was subsequently copied by the Romans and other nations. This is a very broad list covering a long time period and diverse area. For this reason I have included Gallic chariots, although they passed out of use during this period. Caesar encountered chariots for the first time in Britain. I have used the term Gaesatae to describe fanatical warriors inclined to fight naked or 'sky-clad' possibly believing to derive magical protection as a result. Ancient historian Polybius maintains that this is not the name of a tribe but means 'mercenaries'. As with all barbarian lists this one is based on accounts given by their enemies, which like-as-not overemphasise the wild and dangerous nature of these warriors in favour of a good story. We approve, and do not hesitate to fashion our army in the same mould, with warbands of wild fighters, frenzied fanatics, and do-or-die bodyguards.

Search: Brennus, The Battle of Allia, Bituitus King of the Arverni, The Gallic Wars, The Battle of Arar, Ambiorix of the Eburones, Vercingetorix, The Battle of Alesia.

A Gallic warband clashes with Roman legionaries.

Infantry 75%+	At least three quarters of the units in the army must be infantry other than skirmishers.
Warbands 50%+ of infantry	At least half the non-skirmisher infantry units in the army must be medium infantry warbands of one kind or other.
Cavalry up to 25%	Up to a quarter of the units in the army can be cavalry.
Chariots up to 10% if no medium cavalry	Up to one in ten of the army can be chariots so long as the army contains no medium cavalry.
Divisions 4+ units.	Divisions must contain at least 4 units excluding skirmishers and be led by a commander. If general's guard is fielded these must form part of the general's division. If German allies are included they must form a division together with any skirmishers as noted below.
Skirmishers per division 50% of infantry	Divisions may contain up to half as many skirmisher units as they contain non-skirmisher infantry.

Gallic Troop Values

Unit	Clash	Sustained	Short Range	Long Range	Morale Save	Stamina	Special	Points Value
Medium infantry warband armed with swords and javelins	9	6	2	0	5+	6	Wild fighters	28 per unit
• Extra to field warbands as large units	11	8	3	0	5+	8	Wild fighters	+7 per unit
• Extra to field standard-sized warbands as Belgae	9	6	2	0	5+	6	Wild fighters, Eager	Free
• Extra to field standard-sized warbands as German allies – up to 4 units	9	6	2	0	5+	6	Wild fighters, Brave	+3 per unit
• Extra to field a standard-sized warband as Gaesatae – up to 1 unit	9	6	2	0	5+	6	Wild fighters, Fanatic, Frenzied charge	+4 per unit
General's guard medium infantry warband – up to 1 unit	9	6	2	0	5+	6	Tough fighters, Stubborn, Valiant	31 per unit
Skirmishers with javelins fielded as small units	3	2	2	0	0	4		11 per unit
• Extra to equip up to half the skirmisher units with either slings or bows	2	2	2	2	0	4		+1 per unit
Medium cavalry armed with spears/javelins	8	5	3	0	5+	6	Tough fighters	28 per unit
Light cavalry armed with javelins fielded as small units	5	3	2	0	6+	4		17 per unit
Gallic light chariots	6	5	4	0	4+	6		27 per unit
Commanders		1 commander must be provided per division. All commanders including general have leadership 8.						Free

The Illyrians lived in the western Balkans but they left no significant account of themselves. This list has therefore been put together on the evidence of the Illyrians' Roman and Greek adversaries. It covers the period from the near unification of Illyria under King Bardyllis and his wars against the Macedonians, to the final conquest by the Romans and incorporation into the Empire as the province of Illyicum. In the 4th century BC the Illyrians fought against and were defeated by Sparta when they fielded two thousand Greek hoplites as well as a number of their own troops with Greek arms and armour. I have not included these as they were confined to that specific conflict – see the Hoplite list for suitable stats. Illyrians had few cavalry and were masters of raids, ambuscades and skirmishing. Their infantry fought as dense bodies armed with spears, although it's impossible to determine with what degree of discipline. I have chosen to portray them as warbands, but with a modest clash value compared to their northern neighbours. You may prefer to treat them as medium infantry with standard stats, that being an equally valid interpretation. Of special note is the presence of armed slaves amongst the Illyrian forces. I have treated these as levies.

Search: Illyrian Wars, King Bardyllis, Dardanians, Queen Teuta, Battle of Sellasia, King Gentius, Illyrian Warfare.

Cavalry up to 10%	Up to one in ten of the units in the army can be cavalry.
Infantry 75%+	At least three quarters of the units in the army must be infantry other than skirmishers.
Warbands 75%+	At least three quarters of the non-skirmisher infantry must be warbands of one kind or another.
Bow armed skirmishers up to 25% of skirmishers	Up to a quarter of the skirmisher units can be bow armed – the remainder must be armed with javelins or slings.
Divisions 4+ units	Divisions must contain at least 4 units excluding skirmishers and must be led by a commander. One division can consist entirely of skirmishers, but must still contain at least 4 units.
Skirmishers per division 50% of infantry	Mixed divisions may contain up to half as many skirmisher units as they contain non-skirmisher infantry. If general's guard is fielded these must form part of the general's division. A division that consists entirely of skirmishers cannot include more that half the total number of skirmish units in the army.

Illyrian Troop Values

Unit	Combat				Morale Save	Stamina	Special	Points Value
	Clash	Sustained	Short Range	Long Range				
Medium cavalry with javelins – up to 1 unit	8	5	3	0	5+	6		27 per unit
Light cavalry armed with javelins and fielded as small units	5	3	2	0	6+	4		17 per unit
Medium infantry warband armed with javelins or spears	7	6	2	0	5+	6		23 per unit
• *Extra to make medium infantry warband tough fighters – up to half*	8	6	2	0	5+	6	*Tough fighters, Eager*	*+2 per unit*
• *Extra to make medium infantry warband tough fighters and frenzied – up to half*	8	6	2	0	5+	6	*Tough fighters, Frenzied charge*	*+5 per unit*
• *Reduction to field medium infantry warband as armed slaves – up to half*	6	5	2	0	5+	6	*Levy*	*–5 per unit*
Medium infantry warband general's guard – up to 1 unit	8	6	2	0	5+	6	Tough fighters, Stubborn	27 per unit
Light infantry armed with javelins and shields	5	5	3	0	6+	6		20 per unit
Light infantry archers	4	4	3	3	0	6		20 per unit
• *Reduction to field light infantry archers as small units*	3	3	2	2	0	4		*–6 per unit*
Skirmishers with javelins fielded as small units	3	2	2	0	0	4		11 per unit
Skirmishers with slings fielded as small units	2	2	2	2	0	4		12 per unit
Skirmishers with bows fielded as small units	2	2	2	2	0	4		12 per unit
• *Extra to make sling or bow-armed skirmishers marksmen – up to half of each*	2	2	2	2	0	4	*Marksmen*	*+1 per unit*
Commanders	1 commander must be provided per division. All commanders including general have leadership 8.							Free

This is the army that opposed Alexander the Great and his Macedonians during his conquest of the Persian Empire. It has obvious similarities to the earlier armies of Xerxes and Darius I, although it draws upon the accounts of Alexander's victories for its sources. The Persians have good cavalry and mercenary Greeks, but the Persian infantry are poor quality and not likely to withstand the advance of the Macedonians for very long. As already explained in the list for Early Achaemenid Persians, the spara is the tall, oblong shield carried by spear-armed and mixed Persian infantry units. It was often used to form an improvised barrier. This is represented by allowing the –1 to hit by ranged fire from the front in the same way as for formations of heavy infantry. No point cost has been allocated for this and the rule can be ignored for units that do not carry it should players wish.

Search: Artaxerxes III, Darius III, The Battle of Granicus, The Battle of Issus, The Battle of Gaugamela.

Cavalry up to 50%	Up to half the units in the army can be cavalry.
Infantry 25%+	At least a quarter of the units in the army must be infantry other than skirmishers.
Heavy scythed chariots up to 3	The army can include up to 3 heavy scythed chariots.
Divisions 4+ units	Divisions must contain at least 4 units excluding skirmishers and must be led by a commander. If mercenary Greeks are included these must form their own exclusively Greek division(s) led by a Greek commander. These may include skirmishers as noted below.
Skirmishers per division 50% of infantry	Divisions may contain up to half as many skirmisher units as they contain non-skirmisher infantry.

Later Achaemenid Persian Troop Values

Unit	Clash	Sustained	Short Range	Long Range	Morale Save	Stamina	Special	Points Value
Guard medium infantry with spears – up to 1 unit	6	6	3	0	5+	6	Stubborn, Sparabara (see notes)	25 per unit
• Extra to give guard spears and bows	6	6	3	3	5+	6	Stubborn, Marksmen, Sparabara (see notes)	+4 per unit
Levy medium infantry with spears – up to 1 unit	6	6	3	0	5+	6	Levy, Sparabara (see notes)	20 per unit
• Extra to give medium infantry bows in addition	6	6	3	3	5+	6	Levy, Sparabara (see notes)	+3 per unit
Levy medium infantry armed with bows	5	5	3	3	5+	6	Levy	21 per unit
• Reduction to make bow-armed levy militia – up to half	5	5	3	3	5+	6	Levy, Militia	-3 per unit
Greek mercenary hoplite heavy infantry armed with long spears	7	7	3/0	0	4+	6	Elite, Phalanx	35 per unit
Greek mercenary light infantry peltasts with spears/javelins	5	5	3	0	6+	6		20 per unit
• Reduction to field peltasts as small units	3	3	2	0	6+	4		–7 per unit
Skirmishers with javelins fielded as small units	3	2	2	0	0	4		11 per unit
• Extra to give skirmishers slings instead of javelins – up to half the skirmisher units	2	2	2	2	0	4		+1 per unit
• Extra to give skirmishers bows instead of javelins – up to half the skirmisher units	2	2	2	2	0	4		+2 per unit
• Reduction to field any skirmisher units as levy regardless of armament	————————— As above —————————						Levy	–2 per unit
Light cavalry armed with javelins fielded as small units	5	3	2	0	6+	4	Feigned flight	19 per unit
• Extra to replace light cavalry javelins with bows – up to half	5	3	2	2	6+	4	Feigned flight	+2 per unit
• Reduction to field any light cavalry units as levy regardless of armament	————————— As above —————————						Levy	–4 per unit
Horse archers fielded as small units	4	2	2	2	6+	4	Parthian shot	19 per unit
Guard heavy cavalry with spears – up to 1 unit	9	6	3	0	4+	6	Stubborn	33 per unit

Unit	Combat				Morale Save	Stamina	Special	Points Value
	Clash	Sustained	Short Range	Long Range				
Medium cavalry armed with spears	8	5	3	0	5+	6		27 per unit
• Extra to upgrade medium cavalry to heavy cavalry – up to half	9	6	3	0	4+	6		+3 per unit
○ Extra to give a unit of heavy cavalry spears and bows – up to 1 unit	9	6	3	2	4+	6		+2 per unit
• Reduction to make above heavy or medium cavalry levy – up to half			As above				Levy	–3 per unit
Heavy scythed chariots fielded as units of 1 model	7	0	0	0	3+	4	Scythed chariot	10 per unit
Commanders		1 commander must be provided per division. All commanders including general have leadership 7.						Free
• Extra to upgrade commanders other than the general to leadership 8 – up to half								+10 each

ALEXANDRIAN MACEDONIAN

Late 4th century BC

This list represents the army of Alexander the Great, his father Philip, and his immediate successors during the years after his death. It features the pike phalanx – a development of the long-spear phalanx adopted from the Thebans by Philip who had probably witnessed the Thebans fighting whilst held hostage there. The army is built around its core of Macedonian phalangites and elite Companion cavalry led by Alexander himself. The option to replace cavalry spears/javelins with lances represents the Macedonian xyston in cases where players feel they want to make the distinction between this longer and heavier weapon and the lighter spears carried by opposing horsemen. Where any cavalry are equipped with lances, all Agema/Companion cavalry should be so equipped as this was their favoured weapon. Note that the rules designation of 'medium cavalry' is usual for heavy cavalry types of the classical era – no slight is intended upon the prowess of the Companions! Hypaspists are represented as pike-armed; however, views do vary on this and players wishing to field them with long spears can do so with the same stats and points values.

Search: Alexander the Great, the Battle of Granicus, The Battle of Issus, The Siege of Tyre, The Battle of Gaugamela, The Battle of the Hydaspes.

Phalangites ready for action.

Infantry 50%+	At least half the units in the army must be made up of infantry other than skirmishers.
Cavalry up to 50%	Up to half of the units in the army can be cavalry.
Pike 25%+ of infantry	At least a quarter of the non-skirmisher infantry units in the army must comprise pike-armed phalanx of one type or another.
Artillery 1 of each type up to 10%	Up to one unit of each type and no more than one in ten of the number of units in the army in total.
Divisions 4+ units	Divisions must contain at least 4 units excluding skirmishers and be led by a commander. If the Hetairoi Companion guard is fielded these must form part of the general's division.
Skirmishers per division 50% of infantry	Divisions may contain up to half as many skirmisher units as they contain non-skirmisher infantry.

Unit	Clash	Sustained	Short Range	Long Range	Morale Save	Stamina	Special	Points Value
Phalangite heavy infantry armed with pikes	7	7	3/0	0	4+	6	Phalanx	32 per unit
• Extra to upgrade phalanx to veteran – up to half	7	7	3/0	0	4+	6	Drilled, Phalanx	+3 per unit
• Extra to upgrade phalanx to Hypaspists – 1 unit only	7	7	3/0	0	4+	6	Drilled, Phalanx, Stubborn, Elite	+9 per unit
Mercenary hoplite heavy infantry armed with long spears	7	7	3/0	0	4+	6	Elite, Phalanx	35 per unit
Light infantry peltasts with spears/javelins	5	5	3	0	6+	6		20 per unit
• Extra to field light infantry peltasts as Thracians with double-handed rhomphaia – 1 unit only	6	5	2/0	0	6+	6	Tough fighters	+2 per unit
• Reduction to field light infantry peltasts with spears/javelin as small units	3	3	2	0	6+	4		–7 per unit
Skirmishers armed with javelins and fielded as small units	3	2	2	0	0	4		11 per unit
• Extra to give skirmishers slings instead of javelins – up to half the skirmisher units	2	2	2	2	0	4		+1 per unit
◦ Extra to upgrade skirmisher slingers to Rhodians – 1 unit only	2	2	2	2	0	4	Marksmen	+1 per unit
• Extra to give skirmishers bows instead of javelins – 1 unit only	2	2	2	2	0	4		+1 per unit
◦ Extra to upgrade skirmisher bowmen to Cretans	2	2	2	2	0	4	Marksmen	+1 per unit
Companion medium cavalry armed with spears	9	6	3	0	5+	6	Drilled, Elite	35 per unit
• Extra to give Companions lances instead of spears	9	6	3/0	0	5+	6	Drilled, Elite	+3 per unit
• Extra to upgrade Companions to Hetairoi regardless of armament– up to 1 unit	——— As above ———						Drilled, Elite, Tough fighters, Stubborn	+3 per unit
Thessalian medium cavalry armed with spears	8	5	3	0	5+	6	Drilled	30 per unit
• Extra to give Thessalian medium cavalry lances instead of spears	8	5	3/0	0	5+	6	Drilled	+3 per unit
Thracian or Thessalian light cavalry armed with javelins and fielded as small units	5	3	2	0	6+	4		17 per unit
• Extra to give Thessalian light cavalry lances instead of javelins – up to 1 unit	5	3	2/0	0	6+	4		+2 per unit
• Extra to give non lance-armed Thracian or Thessalian light cavalry feigned flight	5	3	2	0	6+	4	Feigned flight	+2 per unit
Light artillery bolt throwers	1	1	2	2	0	3		15 per unit
Medium artillery onagers	1	1	0	3	0	3		20 per unit
Heavy artillery ballistas	1	1	0	3	0	3		23 per unit
Commanders	1 commander must be provided per division. All commanders including general have leadership 8.							Free
• Extra to upgrade general to Alexander	If the army includes Hetairoi Companion guard it can be led by Alexander the Great. Alexander the Great has leadership 9 and can add up to a maximum of 6 attacks in hand-to-hand combat instead of the usual 3.							+25

THE WAR OF FIRE

The war between the Romans and the Celtiberians was called the 'War of Fire', so remarkable was the uninterrupted character of the engagements... Winter alone put a check on the progress of the war and on the continuous character of the battles, so that on the whole if we can conceive a war to be fiery it would be this and no other.

Polybius

Egyptian Middle Kingdom 'Eye Axe'
c. 19th Century BC (Perry Collection)

This is the army with which the first emperor Qin Shi Huang united all of China for the first time. It is also the army represented by the famous Terracotta Army found just outside Xi'an in Shaanxi Province. This provides us with a detailed 1:1 model of the actual army to use as the basis for our reconstruction – if only other rulers of ancient times had been so considerate! The option to field troops as fanatics is based on an account of Qin infantry as so keen to get to grips that they threw away their armour and spears. This is more than a tad unlikely, but rather colourful! Wu Hu refers to the five horse-riding barbarian tribes of the north (it means Five Barbarians). The term is strictly speaking anachronistic but it's a useful generic description. The Chinese were poor horsemen and the Qin, whose borders lay next to these tribes, were the first to adopt a cavalry arm in response. The ji is a rather unusual looking spear with a second head set at right angles to the first; it seems unnecessary to burden the army with special rules on account of this, so treat it the same as a regular spear or javelin. Crossbowmen are common amongst the figures in the Terracotta Army and I have described both bowmen and crossbowmen as archers. I would suggest these relatively light crossbows be treated as bows, but players can apply the crossbow rule if they prefer with no points adjustment. Chariots are classed as light chariots making them quite manoeuvrable, but combine the fighting stats of heavier chariots because of the four-horse team and larger crew – this is deliberate!

Search: Shang Yang, The Warring States Period, King Zheng, Qin Shi Huang, The First Emperor of China, The Terracotta Army.

Infantry 50%+	At least half the units in the army must be infantry other than skirmishers.
Cavalry up to 25%	Up to a quarter of the units in the army can be cavalry.
Chariots up to 10%	Up to one in ten units in the army can be chariots.
Divisions 4+ units	Divisions must contain at least 4 units excluding skirmishers and must be led by a commander.
Skirmishers per division 50% of infantry	Divisions may contain up to half as many skirmisher units as they contain non-skirmisher infantry.

Qin China Troop Values

Unit	Clash	Sustained	Short Range	Long Range	Morale Save	Stamina	Special	Points Value
Heavy infantry armed with ji spears and swords	7	7	3	0	4+	6	Drilled	29 per unit
• Extra to upgrade heavy infantry to veteran – up to half in total	7	7	3	0	4+	6	Drilled, Elite	+3 per unit
• Extra to incorporate archers into rear ranks of heavy infantry and/or veterans	7	7	3	2	4+	6	As above	+2 per unit
Medium infantry armed with ji spears and swords	6	6	3	0	5+	6	Drilled	26 per unit
• Extra to incorporate archers into rear ranks	6	6	3	2	5+	6	Drilled	+2 per unit
• Reduction to field either of the above as undrilled impressed troops	——— As above ———							–3 per unit
° Reduction to make impressed troops convicts	——— As above ———						Levy	–3 per unit
• Extra to field medium infantry with ji spears and swords only as fanatic – up to half	6	6	3/0	0	5+	6	Wild fighters, Fanatic, Frenzied charge	+4 per unit
Light infantry with spears and/or javelins	5	5	3	0	6+	6		20 per unit
Light infantry archers with bows or crossbows	4	4	3	3	6+	6		21 per unit
• Reduction to field light infantry archers as small unit	3	3	2	2	6+	4		–6 per unit
Skirmishers armed with javelins and fielded as small units	3	2	2	0	0	4		11 per unit
Skirmishers armed with bows or crossbows and fielded as small units	2	2	2	2	0	4		12 per unit
Medium cavalry with spear and/or javelins	8	5	3	0	5+	6		27 per unit
Wu Hu light cavalry armed with javelins and bows and fielded as small units	5	3	2	2	6+	4	Feigned flight	21 per unit
Wu Hu horse archers fielded as small units	4	2	2	2	6+	4	Parthian shot	19 per unit

Qin China Troop Values

Unit	Combat				Morale Save	Stamina	Special	Points Value
	Clash	Sustained	Short Range	Long Range				
Qin horse archers with bows or crossbows – fielded as small units	4	2	2	2	6+	4		17 per unit
Four-horse light chariots with crews armed with crossbows and spears	9	5	3	3	4+	6		32 per unit
Commanders	1 commander must be provided per division. All commanders including general have leadership 8.							Free
• Extra to upgrade general to leadership 9	The general can have leadership 9 at the following extra cost.							+25

ALEXANDER'S SUCCESSORS
Late 4th-3rd centuries BC

This list represents the armies of the Successor States as they developed in the generation following Alexander's death. At heart they remain similar to the earlier army of conquest. Indeed, the same warriors continued to fight on under new masters, often into old age. Alexander's Successors were quick to make use of native troops where they were available, especially in the form of elephants and cavalry. The option to replace cavalry spears/javelins with lances represents the Macedonian xyston in cases where players feel they want to make the distinction between this longer and heavier weapon and lighter spears carried by opposing horsemen. Where any cavalry are equipped with lances, all Agema/Companion cavalry should be so equipped as this was their favoured weapon.

Search: Perdiccas, Craterus, Antipater, Ptolemy, Lysimachus, Antigonus, Seleucus.

Infantry 50%+	At least half the units in the army must be infantry other than skirmishers.
Cavalry up to 50%	Up to half of the units in the army can be cavalry.
Pike 25%+ of infantry	At least a quarter of the non-skirmisher infantry units in the army must comprise pike-armed phalanx of one type or another.
Artillery 1 of each type up to 10%	The army can include up to one unit of each type and no more than one in ten of the number of units in the army in total.
Elephants up to 10%	Up to one in ten units in the army can be elephants.
Divisions 4+ units	Divisions must contain at least 4 units excluding skirmishers and must be led by a commander.
Skirmishers per division 50% of infantry	Divisions may contain up to half as many skirmisher units as they contain non-skirmisher infantry.

Alexander's Successors Troop Values

Unit	Combat				Morale Save	Stamina	Special	Points Value
	Clash	Sustained	Short Range	Long Range				
Phalangite heavy infantry armed with pikes	7	7	3/0	0	4+	6	Phalanx	32 per unit
• Extra to upgrade phalanx to veteran – up to half	7	7	3/0	0	4+	6	Drilled, Phalanx	+3 per unit
• Extra to upgrade phalanx to guard – 1 unit only	7	7	3/0	0	4+	6	Drilled, Phalanx, Elite, Stubborn	+9 per unit
Mercenary hoplite heavy infantry armed with long spears	7	7	3/0	0	4+	6	Elite, Phalanx	35 per unit
Light infantry with spears/javelins	5	5	3	0	6+	6		20 per unit
• Extra to field light infantry as Thracians with double-handed rhomphaia – 1 unit only	6	5	2/0	0	6+	6	Tough fighters	+2 per unit
• Reduction to field light infantry as small units	3	3	2	0	6+	4		−7 per unit

Unit	Combat				Morale Save	Stamina	Special	Points Value
	Clash	Sustained	Short Range	Long Range				
Skirmishers armed with javelins and fielded as small units	3	2	2	0	0	4		11 per unit
• Extra to give skirmishers slings instead of javelins – up to half the skirmisher units	2	2	2	2	0	4		+1 per unit
○ Extra to upgrade skirmisher slingers to Rhodians – 1 unit only	2	2	2	2	0	4	Marksmen	+1 per unit
• Extra to give skirmishers bows instead of javelins – up to half	2	2	2	2	0	4		+1 per unit
○ Extra to upgrade skirmisher bowmen to Cretans	2	2	2	2	0	4	Marksmen	+1 per unit
Companion or Agema medium cavalry armed with spears	9	6	3	0	5+	6	Drilled, Elite	35 per unit
• Extra to upgrade Companion or Agema medium cavalry to heavy cavalry	9	6	3	0	4+	6	Drilled, Elite	+1 per unit
• Extra to give Companions or Agema medium or heavy cavalry lances instead of spears	9	6	3/0	0	As above	6	Drilled, Elite	+3 per unit
Line medium cavalry armed with spears	8	5	3	0	5+	6	Drilled	30 per unit
• Extra to give line cavalry lances instead of spears	8	5	3/0	0	5+	6	Drilled	+3 per unit
Light cavalry armed with javelins and fielded as small units	5	3	2	0	6+	4		17 per unit
• Extra to give light cavalry lances instead of javelins – up to 1 unit	5	3	2/0	0	6+	4		+2 per unit
• Extra to give non lance-armed light cavalry feigned flight	5	3	2	0	6+	4	Feigned flight	+2 per unit
Elephant with javelin-armed crew	4	3	1	0	4+	6	Elephant	23 per unit
Light infantry elephant guard as small units – up to 1 per elephant	3	3	2	0	6+	4	Sub-unit of elephant	13 per unit
Light artillery bolt throwers	1	1	2	2	0	3		15 per unit
Medium artillery onagers	1	1	0	3	0	3		20 per unit
Heavy artillery ballistas	1	1	0	3	0	3		23 per unit
Commanders	1 commander must be provided per division. All commanders including general have leadership 8.							Free
• Extra to upgrade general to leadership 9	The general can have leadership 9 at the following extra cost.							+25
• Extra to upgrade other commanders to leadership 9 – up to half	Other commanders can have leadership 9 at the following extra cost.							+15

Lightly equipped peltasts skirmish ahead of the Greek phalanx.

This list represents Greek armies of the period following the Macedonian conquest and up until the Roman occupation. This is an army of transition that saw the hoplite gradually replaced by thureophoroi/thorakitai and eventually by the pike-armed phalanx. Some Greek states were slower to make this transition than others, but the high days of the hoplite were well and truly over, and soon even the most hidebound were to abandon what had been one of the most successful fighting methods of ancient times.

Key words: The Achaean League, The Aetolian League, The Battle of Corinth 146 BC.

Infantry 75%+	At least three quarters of units in the army must be infantry other than skirmishers.
Cavalry up to 25%	Up to a quarter of the units in the army can be cavalry.
Divisions 4+ units	Divisions must contain at least 4 units excluding skirmishers and must be led by a commander.
Skirmishers per division 50% of infantry	Divisions may contain up to half as many skirmisher units as they contain non-skirmisher infantry.

Hellenistic Greek Troop Values

Unit	Clash	Sustained	Short Range	Long Range	Morale Save	Stamina	Special	Points Value
Hoplite heavy infantry armed with long spears	7	7	3/0	0	4+	6	Phalanx, Drilled	35 per unit
Thorakitai heavy infantry with spears and javelins	7	7	3	0	4+	6	Drilled	29 per unit
Thureophoroi medium infantry with spears and javelins	6	6	3	0	5+	6	Drilled	26 per unit
Phalangite heavy infantry with pikes	7	7	3/0	0	4+	6	Phalanx, Drilled	35 per unit
Aetolian, Illyrian or similar peltast-type light infantry armed with spears and javelins	5	5	3	0	6+	6		20 per unit
• *Reduction to field light infantry as small units*	3	3	2	0	6+	4		*–7 per unit*
Skirmishers armed with javelins and fielded as small units	3	2	2	0	0	4		11 per unit
• *Extra to give skirmishers slings instead of javelins – up to half the skirmisher units*	2	2	2	2	0	4		*+1 per unit*
• *Extra to give skirmishers bows instead of javelins – up to 1 unit*	2	2	2	2	0	4		*+1 per unit*
° *Extra to upgrade bowmen to Cretans*	2	2	2	2	0	4	*Marksmen*	*+1 per unit*
Medium cavalry armed with spears and/or javelins	8	5	3	0	5+	6		27 per unit
• *Upgrade medium cavalry to guard – up to 1 unit*	8	5	3	0	5+	6	*Elite*	*+3 per unit*
Thracian or Aetolian light cavalry armed with javelins and fielded as small units	5	3	2	0	6+	4	Feigned flight	19 per unit
• *Upgrade light cavalry to Tarentines – up to 1 unit*	5	3	2	0	6+	4	*Feigned flight, Elite*	*+2 per unit*
Light artillery bolt throwers	1	1	2	2	0	3		15 per unit
Commanders			1 commander must be provided per division. All commanders including general have leadership 8.					Free

> "They were the first Greeks, as far as I know, to charge at a run, and the first to dare to look without flinching at Persian dress and the men who wore it; for until that day came, no Greek could hear even the word Persian without terror."
>
> Herodotus on the Battle of Marathon

This list covers the easternmost of the Bactrian and Graeco-Indian Successor states in what is today Uzbekistan, Afghanistan, Pakistan and North West India. Here a Greek aristocracy ruled over a native population for many generations, creating a synthesis of Greek and Indian cultures that was to profoundly influence art styles and philosophical thinking in the sub-continent. These states fought amongst themselves as well as against their neighbours, and were eventually conquered by invading Scythians and absorbed into the succeeding Indo-Scythian empire. Light cavalry could be Bactrians, Arachosians or similar native horse. Skirmishers could be Greek colonists or native types.

Key words: Diodotus I, Ariana, Greco-Bactrian Kingdoms, Indo-Greek Kingdoms.

Infantry 25%+	At least a quarter of units in the army must be infantry other than skirmishers.
Cavalry 25%+	At least a quarter of units in the army must be cavalry.
Chariots up to 10%	Up to one in ten of the units in the army can be chariots.
Elephants up to 20%	Up to one in five of the units in the army can be elephants.
Divisions 4+ units	Divisions must contain at least 4 units excluding skirmishers and must be led by a commander. If the guard cavalry unit is fielded it must form part of the general's division.
Skirmishers per division 50% of infantry	Divisions may contain up to half as many skirmisher units as they contain non-skirmisher infantry.

Bactrian Greek Troop Values

Unit	Combat				Morale Save	Stamina	Special	Points Value
	Clash	Sustained	Short Range	Long Range				
Phalangite heavy infantry with pikes	7	7	3/0	0	4+	6	Phalanx, Drilled	35 per unit
Peltast or native light infantry armed with spears and javelins	5	5	3	0	6+	6		20 per unit
• *Reduction to field light infantry as small units*	3	3	2	0	6+	4		–7 *per unit*
Indian medium infantry with mixed ranks of spears/javelins and bows	6	6	3	3	5+	6		26 per unit
Indian medium infantry armed with bows	5	5	3	3	5+	6		24 per unit
Skirmishers armed with javelins and fielded as small units	3	2	2	0	0	4		11 per unit
Skirmishers armed with slings and fielded as small units	2	2	2	2	0	4		12 per unit
Skirmishers armed with bows and fielded as small units	2	2	2	2	0	4		12 per unit
Greek medium cavalry armed with spears and/or javelins	8	5	3	0	5+	6		27 per unit
Greek/Bactrian heavy cavalry armed with spears and/or javelins	9	6	3	0	4+	6		30 per unit
• *Upgrade heavy cavalry to guard cavalry – up to 1 unit*	9	6	3	0	4+	6	Elite	+3 *per unit*
Saka heavy cavalry with bows and kontos – up to 1 unit	9	6	3	2	4+	6		35 per unit
Saka horse archers fielded as small units	4	2	2	2	6+	4	Parthian shot	19 per unit
Indian medium cavalry armed with spears and/or javelins	8	5	3	0	5+	6		27 per unit
Light cavalry armed with javelins and fielded as small units	5	3	2	0	6+	4	Feigned flight	19 per unit
Light cavalry armed with javelins and bows fielded as small units	5	3	2	2	6+	4	Feigned flight	21 per unit
Elephant with crew armed with spears, javelins and bows	4	3	1	1	4+	6	Elephant	24 per unit
Heavy chariots carrying crews with mixed arms	9	5	3	3	3+	6		33 per unit
Commanders	1 commander must be provided per division. All commanders including general have leadership 8.							Free

This is the army that gave the Romans such a terrible fright and forever established the name of Hannibal as one of the greatest generals of all time. It is a force that combines many different types of troops including allies and mercenaries and, of course, elephants. Hannibal's army terrorised Italy, and it was only the threat of fresh Roman armies back home in Africa that finally forced the wily commander to return to defend Carthage itself. I have not placed any restriction on which troops can be formed together into divisions, although historically Gauls, Spaniards and Italians fought in their own native contingents. Players will no doubt wish to organise their forces along these lines where practical, but to impose a restriction would make it very difficult to put together average-sized armies. Note that light cavalry can be Liby-phoenician, Gallic, Spanish, Numidians or Italians. Skirmishers are likely to be any of these.

Search: The Punic Wars, Hannibal, the Battles of Trebia, Trasimene, Cannae and Zama, The Mercenary War, Battle of the Saw.

Infantry 66%+	At least two thirds of units in the army must be infantry excluding skirmishers.
Libyan spearmen up to 25% of infantry	Up to one in four of the non-skirmishing infantry units can be Libyan spearmen.
Cavalry up to 25%	Up to a quarter of the units in the army can be cavalry.
Light cavalry 50%+ of cavalry	At least half of the cavalry units in the army must be light cavalry.
Elephants up to 10%	Up to one in ten units in the army can be elephants.
Divisions 4+ units	Divisions must contain at least 4 units excluding skirmishers and must be led by a commander.
Skirmishers per division 50% of infantry	Divisions may contain up to half as many skirmisher units as they contain non-skirmisher infantry.

Carthaginian Troop Values

Unit	Clash	Sustained	Short Range	Long Range	Morale Save	Stamina	Special	Points Value
Libyan heavy infantry with long spears	7	7	3/0	0	4+	6		29 per unit
• Extra to upgrade Libyan heavy infantry with long spears to veterans	7	7	3/0	0	4+	6	Elite, Phalanx, Tough fighters	+7 per unit
Gallic medium infantry warband armed with swords and javelins	9	6	2	0	5+	6	Wild fighters	28 per unit
• Extra to field medium infantry warbands as large units	11	8	3	0	5+	8	Wild fighters	+7 per unit
Italian allied medium infantry armed with spears or javelins	6	6	3	0	5+	6		23 per unit
Celtiberian medium infantry warband armed with pila	9	6	2	0	5+	6		28 per unit
Spanish scutarii medium infantry armed with pila	6	6	3	0	5+	6		23 per unit
Spanish caetrati light infantry with javelins and fielded as small units	3	3	2	0	0	4		12 per unit
Ligurian light infantry armed with javelins	5	5	3	0	6+	6		20 per unit
Skirmishers armed with javelins and fielded as small units	3	2	2	0	0	4		11 per unit
• Extra to give skirmishers slings instead of javelins – up to half the skirmisher units	2	2	2	2	0	4		+1 per unit
○ Extra to upgrade skirmisher slingers to Spanish Balearic – up to 1 unit	2	2	2	2	0	4	Marksmen	+1 per unit
• Extra to give skirmishers bows instead of javelins as Numidians – up to 1 unit	2	2	2	2	0	4		+1 per unit
Liby-Phoenician medium cavalry fielded as small units	6	3	2	0	5+	4		19 per unit
• Extra to make cavalry guard – up to 1 unit	6	3	2	0	5+	4	Elite	+2 per unit

Unit	Combat Clash	Combat Sustained	Combat Short Range	Combat Long Range	Morale Save	Stamina	Special	Points Value
Light cavalry armed with javelins and fielded as small units	5	3	2	0	6+	4		17 per unit
• Extra to upgrade light cavalry to Numidians	5	3	2	0	6+	4	*Feigned flight*	+2 per unit
Gallic/Spanish medium cavalry allies	8	5	3	0	5+	6		27 per unit
• Extra to upgrade cavalry allies to tough fighters – up to 1 unit	8	5	3	0	5+	6	*Tough fighters*	+1 per unit
Elephant with javelin-armed crew	4	3	1	0	4+	6	Elephant	23 per unit
Commanders	1 commander must be provided per division. All commanders including general have leadership 8.							Free
• Extra to upgrade general to leadership 9	*The general can have leadership 9 at the following extra cost.*							+25

"The strength of Rome is founded on her ancient customs as much as on the strength of her sons."

Quintus Ennius

REPUBLICAN ROME

3rd–2nd centuries BC

This is the classic army of Rome's wars against Carthage, the Macedonians and Seleucids. It is not dissimilar to the earlier Camillan army, but is replete with allies and mercenaries and overall more varied and interesting. It features the three types of Roman infantry: principes, hastati and triarii who would fight in three lines one behind the other. These troops can be Romans or Latin allies. During the earliest part of the Punic Wars hastati could still be fielded with long spears instead of pila, but I leave it to players to make this adjustment if they feel so inclined. Similarly, the transition of the principes armament from long spears to pila can be accommodated within this list if players wish – it was part of a gradual evolution of Roman arms and difficult to pin down to any exact time. Light cavalry can be Italian, Gallic, Spanish, Illlyrian, Greek or Numidians. Skirmishers can be any of these. The classic Roman three-line fighting formation with hastati at the front, principes behind, and triarii at the rear is difficult to impose upon players who often want to lead with their 'best' troops – namely the triarii. To encourage players to use historical tactics we rule that hastati units don't count for purposes of the division becoming broken. It therefore makes sense to use them for the initial fighting. Triarii, on the other hand, have a support value of 3, being a bonused value for a small unit. As mentioned in the Camillan list we would not quibble with players who prefer to deploy their units as standard sized rather than small if that is their preference, the Marian list has suitable stats for such units. Velites can be represented as skirmishers or light infantry depending upon their experience and effectiveness – suitable stats are included for both as well as other skirmishing infantry. The Greeks, Ligurians, Illyrians and elephants feature in Rome's subsequent wars against Hellenistic armies and are included to represent those forces.

Search: The Punic Wars, Scipio Africanus, The Battle of Zama, The Macedonian War, The Battle of Pydna, The Battle of Magnesia, Battle of Thermopylae (191 BC).

Infantry 75%+	At least three quarters of units in the army must be infantry other than skirmishers.
Hastati, principes and triarii 50% infantry	Together hastati, principes and triarii must make up at least half the units of non-skirmish infantry. Hastati and principes units must be bought in pairs – 1 hastati + 1 principes. Triarii can be included in the ratio of 1 unit of triarii for every 2 pairs of hastati/principes ie 2 hastati: 2 principes: 1 triarii.
Cavalry up to 25%	Up to a quarter of the units in the army can be cavalry.
Light Cavalry at least 50% of cavalry	At least half of the cavalry units in the army must be light cavalry.
Divisions 4+ units	Divisions must contain at least 4 units excluding skirmishers and must be led by a commander. Allied infantry must be fielded in divisions wholly composed of native troops i.e all Gauls, all Spanish, all Italians, all Numidians, all Illyrians, etc. These native divisions can include skirmishers as noted below.
Skirmishers per division 50% of infantry	Divisions may contain up to half as many skirmisher units as they contain non-skirmisher infantry.

Unit	Clash	Sustained	Short Range	Long Range	Morale Save	Stamina	Special	Points Value
Hastati or principes heavy infantry armed with pila and fielded as small units	5	5	2	0	4+	4	Drilled	23 per unit
• *Extra to make hastati tough fighters*	5	5	2	0	4+	4	*Drilled, Tough fighters*	+1 per unit
Principes heavy infantry armed with long spears and fielded as small units	5	5	2/0	0	4+	4	Drilled	23 per unit
• *Extra to make principes with long spears stubborn*	5	5	2/0	0	4+	4	*Drilled, Stubborn*	+2 per unit
• *Reduction to make a pair of hastati/principes in the same division levy*	5	5	2/0	0	4+	4	*Levy*	-8 per pair
Triarii heavy infantry armed with long spears and fielded as small units	5	5	3/0	0	4+	4	Drilled, Elite, Stubborn	28 per unit
• *Extra to make triarii valiant*	5	5	3/0	0	4+	4	*Drilled, Elite, Stubborn, Valiant*	+2 per unit
Italian allied medium infantry armed with spears and/or javelins	6	6	3	0	5+	6		23 per unit
• *Reduction to make allied Italians levy*	6	6	3	0	5+	6	*Levy*	–3 per unit
Gallic or Celtiberian medium infantry warband armed with swords and javelins	9	6	2	0	5+	6	Wild fighters	28 per unit
• *Extra to field medium infantry warbands as large units*	11	8	3	0	5+	8	*Wild fighters*	+7 per unit
Spanish scutarii medium infantry armed with pila	6	6	3	0	5+	6		26 per unit
Illyrian, Greek or Ligurian light infantry with javelins	5	5	3	0	6+	6		20 per unit
Velites or Spanish caetrati light infantry armed with javelins and fielded as small units	3	3	2	0	6+	4		13 per unit
• *Extra to upgrade velites to tough fighters*	3	3	2	0	6+	4	*Tough fighters*	+1 point per unit
Skirmishers armed with javelins and fielded as small units	3	2	2	0	0	4		11 per unit
• *Extra to give skirmishers slings instead of javelins – up to half the skirmisher units*	2	2	2	2	0	4		+1 per unit
◦ *Extra to upgrade slingers to Spanish Balearic – up to 1 unit*	2	2	2	2	0	4	*Marksmen*	+1 per unit
• *Extra to give skirmishers bows instead of javelins as Numidians or Cretan Greeks – up to 1 unit*	2	2	2	2	0	4		+1 per unit
◦ *Extra to upgrade Cretan bow-armed skirmishers to marksmen – up to 1 unit*	2	2	2	2	0	4	*Marksmen*	+1 per unit
Romans, Latins or allied Italian medium cavalry fielded as small units	6	3	2	0	5+	4		19 per unit
Light cavalry armed with javelins and fielded as small units	5	3	2	0	6+	4		17 per unit
• *Extra to upgrade light cavalry to Numidians*	5	3	2	0	6+	4	*Feigned flight*	+2 per unit
• *Extra to upgrade light cavalry to Tarentines*	5	3	2	0	6+	4	*Elite, Stubborn*	+3 per unit
Allied Gallic/Spanish medium cavalry	8	5	3	0	5+	6		27 per unit
• *Extra to upgrade allied medium cavalry ao tough fighters – up to 1 unit*	8	5	3	0	5+	6	*Tough fighters*	+1 per unit
Commanders			1 commander must be provided per division. All commanders including general have leadership 8.					Free
• *Extra to upgrade general to leadership 9*			*The general can have leadership 9 at the following extra cost.*					+25

"Oderint dum metuant! (Let them hate – so long as they fear!)"

The poet Lucius Accius wrote these words which, according to Suetonius, were much quoted by the Emperor Caligula

The Gallic hordes that invaded Greece and Anatolia in the 3rd century BC are generally known as Galatians. They invaded through the Balkans via Pannonia and ravaged Greece, defeating an opposing army at Thermopylae in 279 BC after a hard fought battle during which the Galatians came upon the rear of their enemy by means of a mountain pass. Following this the barbarians, under their mighty chieftain Brennus, sacked Delphi – an outrage that caused forces from all over Greece to mass against them. Brennus and his armies were eventually driven out. The barbarians fell to drunken feasting and soon fell out amongst themselves especially after the death of Brennus who took his own life either by an excess of drink, poison or by stabbing himself.

The Galatians were part of a long-term movement of tribes eastward along the south bank of the Danube through Pannonia and Illyria and into the Balkans. Thessalians and Paeonians also took part in the Galatian invasion of Greece, whilst Cappadocians participated in later wars in Asia Minor. The Galatians were defeated by the Seleucids and settled in the Anatolian highlands. Galatia itself was eventually absorbed into the Roman Empire at which time the Galatians fielded imitation Roman-style legionaries. See the Pontic list for stats for these. By this late date the Galatians had settled down a bit though, so no fanatics or chariots can be included alongside imitation legions. Note that small units of light cavalry can also include Galatians and Paeonians.

Search: Leonnorius, Brennus, The Gallic Invasion of The Balkans, The Battle of Thermopylae 279 BC, The Galatian War, Deiotarus.

Cavalry and light chariots up to 25%	Up to a quarter of the units in the army can be cavalry or light chariots.
Infantry 75%+	At least three quarters of the units in the army must be infantry other than skirmishers.
Warbands 50%+ of infantry	At least half the non-skirmisher infantry units in the army must be medium infantry warbands of one kind or other.
Heavy scythed chariot – up to 1	The army can include up to one heavy scythed chariot.
Divisions 4+ units	Divisions must contain at least 4 units excluding skirmishers and must be led by a commander. If general's guard is fielded these must form part of the general's division.
Skirmishers per division 50% of infantry	Divisions may contain up to half as many skirmisher units as they contain non-skirmisher infantry.

Galatian Troop Values

Unit	Clash	Sustained	Short Range	Long Range	Morale Save	Stamina	Special	Points Value
Medium infantry warband armed with swords and javelins	9	6	2	0	5+	6	Wild fighters	28 per unit
• *Extra to field warbands as large units*	11	8	3	0	5+	8	*Wild fighters*	+7 per unit
• *Extra to field a standard-sized warband as naked fanatics – up to 1 unit*	9	6	2	0	5+	6	*Wild fighters, Fanatic, Frenzied charge*	+4 per unit
General's guard medium infantry warband – up to 1 unit	9	6	2	0	5+	6	Tough fighters, Stubborn, Valiant	31 per unit
Cappadocian or Paeonian light infantry with javelins	5	5	3	0	6+	6		20 per unit
• *Reduction to field Cappadocian or Paeonian light infantry as small units*	3	3	2	0	6+	4		–7 per unit
Skirmishers with javelins fielded as small units	3	2	2	0	0	4		11 per unit
Noble Galatian medium cavalry armed with spears/javelins – up to 1 unit	8	5	3	0	5+	6	Tough fighters	28 per unit
Thessalian or Cappadocian light cavalry	7	5	3	0	6+	6		25 per unit
• *Reduction to field light cavalry as small units*	5	3	2	0	6+	4		–8 per unit
Galatian light chariots – up to 1 unit	6	5	4	0	4+	6		27 per unit
Galatian heavy scythed chariot – fielded as a unit of 1 model	6	0	0	0	4+	4		10 per unit
Commanders		1 commander must be provided per division. All commanders including general have leadership 8.						Free

The Parthians were a nomadic Scythian tribe who took over the eastern Satrapies of the old Achaemenid empire once the Greek hold on the region started to weaken. Over the years their power grew until they came to supplant the Seleucids in all but their western enclave of Syria. They came into conflict with Rome many times, and dealt the Romans one of their most infamous defeats at Carrhae in 53 BC. Roman armies were to invade Parthia many times over the following two hundred years, and each time they were beaten back, often most bloodily. The chief bone of contention between the rival empires was the kingdom of Armenia – sometimes part of the Roman sphere of influence and sometimes under Parthian control. Parthian armies are famously based upon horse archers backed-up by very heavily armoured cataphract cavalry. The Parthians did have infantry – although they were not present at the famous victory of Carrhae leading many people to imagine this was typical. Parthian infantry were levies from the cities of Mesopotamia and the Greek colonies left behind by Alexander and were of generally rather poor quality. The camel baggage has been included to represent the animals used to carry extra arrows for the horse archers as at the battle of Carrhae. If the camel baggage is included all horse archer units count as Marksmen at an extra cost of +1 point per unit.

Search: Arsacids, Surena, Ctesiphon, The Battle of Carrhae 53 BC, Battle of Hormizdegan 224 AD.

Cavalry 75%+	At least three quarters of the units in the army must be cavalry.
Horse archers 75%+ of cavalry	At least three quarters of the cavalry units in the army must be horse archers.
Infantry up to 25%	Up to a quarter of the units in the army can be infantry other than skirmishers.
Divisions 4+ units	Divisions must contain at least 4 units excluding skirmishers and must be led by a commander. If the general's household is fielded these must form part of the general's division.
Skirmishers per division 50% of infantry	Divisions may contain up to half as many skirmisher units as they contain non-skirmisher infantry.

Parthian Troop Values

Unit	Clash	Sustained	Short Range	Long Range	Morale Save	Stamina	Special	Points Value
Cataphract cavalry armed with kontos	9	6	3/0	0	4+	6		34 per unit
• Upgrade cataphract cavalry to general's household – up to 1 unit	9	6	3/0	0	4+	6	Stubborn	+3 per unit
Horse archers fielded as small units	4	2	2	2	6+	4	Parthian shot	19 per unit
Light cavalry armed with javelins fielded as small units	5	3	2	0	6+	4	Feigned flight	19 per unit
Levy medium infantry armed with spears	6	6	3	0	5+	6	Levy	20 per unit
Levy medium infantry archers	5	5	3	3	5+	6	Levy	21 per unit
Light infantry archers	4	4	3	3	0	6		20 per unit
• Reduction to field light infantry archers as small units	3	3	2	2	0	4		−6 per unit
Skirmishers with javelins fielded as small units	3	2	2	0	0	4		11 per unit
Camel baggage fielded as tiny unit – up to 1 unit	1	1	1	1	0	1	See notes	10 per unit and +1 point per horse archer unit
Commanders		1 commander must be provided per division. All commanders including general have leadership 8						Free

"Give me a safe commander – not a rash one!"

Augustus Caesar according to Suetonius

NUMIDIANS

The ancient historian Sallust describes the battles of the Romans and Numidians in great detail. He paints a picture of a mixed rabble with little in the way of formal order or organisation. There is little reason to believe matters were much different during any of Rome's campaigns against the rebellious Numidians. I have therefore chosen to represent the majority of troops as light infantry warbands. These can be represented with a mix of weapons that might include a few bowmen amongst the general mass. Skirmishers are also likely to be mixed, and we'd suggest counting range as for slingers for these mixed units. Arguably, the Numidians were the best light cavalry of the classical world, and we have included upgrades to emphasis this, if desired. The Numidians were Berbers. In skin colour and general appearance they would be the same as their descendants in modern day Morocco, Algeria and Libya.

Search: Syphax, Jugurthine War, Juba of Numidia, Tacfarinas, Berbers, Mauretania.

Infantry 25%+	At least a quarter of units in the army must be infantry other than skirmishers.
Medium/heavy infantry up to 25% of infantry	Up to a quarter of the non-skirmishing infantry units in the army can be medium or heavy infantry.
Cavalry up to 50%	Up to half of the units in the army can be cavalry.
Elephants up to 20%	Up to one in five units in the army can be elephants.
Divisions 4+ units	Divisions must contain at least 4 units excluding skirmishers and must be led by a commander. Guard cavalry must fight as part of the general's division.
Skirmishers per division 100% of infantry	Divisions may contain up to as many skirmisher units as they contain non-skirmisher infantry.

Numidian Troop Values

Unit	Clash	Sustained	Short Range	Long Range	Morale Save	Stamina	Special	Points Value
Medium infantry with spears and shields	6	6	3	0	5+	6		23 per unit
• Extra to upgrade all medium infantry to Roman trained heavy infantry – note this must be either all or none	7	7	3	0	4+	6		+3 per unit
Light infantry warband with mixed arms	5	5	2	2	6+	6	Wild fighters	24 per unit
• Extra to field light infantry warbands as large units	7	7	3	3	6+	8	Wild fighters	+8 per unit
Skirmishers armed with javelins and fielded as small units	3	2	2	0	0	4		11 per unit
Skirmishers with slings or bows and fielded as small units	2	2	2	2	0	4		12 per unit
Light cavalry armed with javelins and fielded as small units	5	3	2	0	6+	4	Feigned flight	19 per unit
• Extra to field light cavalry as elite and tough fighters	5	3	2	0	6+	4	Feigned flight, Elite, Tough fighters	+3 per unit
Gallic/Spanish guard medium cavalry – up to 1 unit	8	5	3	0	5+	6	Tough fighters	28 per unit
Elephants with javelin-armed crews	4	3	1	0	4+	6	Elephant	21 per unit
Commanders								Free

1 commander must be provided per division. All commanders including general have leadership 8

The land of Meroe lay to the south of Egypt in the region formerly known as Kush or Nubia. A remnant of Egyptian civilisation endured in this remote spot for many years once Egypt had fallen to the Greeks. The Romans describe the Meroitic armies that invaded southern Egypt as having the character of armed mobs rather than trained troops. These are represented by light infantry warbands. Light infantry could be native Kushites or nomad raiders such as Blemmye or Nobades subsumed into a Meroitic force. Blemmye were probably the ancestors of the Sudanese Beja or Hadendowa that so troubled the British two millennia later. A large proportion of Meroitic warriors would carry a bow. The Kushites probably supplied elephants to the Ptolemies, but whether they used them in war themselves is a matter of conjecture. I have taken the cheerful option of including them in the list and leave it to players to decide.

Search : Queen Candice Amanirenas, Meroe, Gaius Petronius.

Infantry 50%+	At least half the units in the army must be infantry other than skirmishers.
Cavalry up to 25%	Up to a quarter of the units in the army can be cavalry.
Elephants up to 10%	Up to one in ten units in the army can be elephants.
Divisions 4+ units	Divisions must contain at least 4 units excluding skirmishers and must be led by a commander. Guard must belong to the general's division.
Skirmishers per division 50% of infantry	Divisions may contain up to half as many skirmisher units as they contain non-skirmisher infantry.

Meroitic Kushite Troop Values

Unit	Combat				Morale Save	Stamina	Special	Points Value
	Clash	Sustained	Short Range	Long Range				
Medium infantry bodyguard with spears and/or javelins – up to 1 unit	6	6	3	0	5+	6	Tough fighters	24 per unit
• Extra to replace spear-armed guard with medium infantry bow-armed guard	6	6	3	3	5+	6	Marksmen	+3 per unit
Light infantry warband with mixed arms	5	5	2	2	6+	6	Wild fighters, Levy	21 per unit
• Extra to field warbands as large units	7	7	3	3	6+	8	Wild fighters, Levy	+7 per unit
Light infantry archers	4	4	3	3	0	6		20 per unit
Light infantry with spears and/or javelins	5	5	3	0	6+	6		20 per unit
Skirmishers armed with javelins and fielded as small units	3	2	2	0	0	4		11 per unit
Skirmishers with bows and fielded as small unit	2	2	2	2	0	4		12 per unit
Kushite or Nobadian light cavalry armed with spears and/or javelins	7	5	3	0	6+	6	Feigned flight	28 per unit
Kushite or Nobadian light cavalry armed with javelins and fielded as small units	5	3	2	0	6+	4	Feigned flight	19 per unit
Nobadian camel-mounted light cavalry with javelins – fielded as small units	4	3	2	0	6+	4	Feigned flight	18 per unit
Elephant with javelin and bow-armed crew	4	3	1	1	4+	6	Elephant	24 per unit
Commanders	1 commander must be provided per division. The general has leadership of 8. Other commanders have leadership 7.							Free

> "I had rather excel in the knowledge of what is excellent, than in the extent of my power and dominion."
>
> Alexander the Great

Rome's wars in Spain lasted throughout the period of the Punic Wars and beyond. The eastern part of Spain became the chief region of conflict between the growing powers of Carthage and the Roman Republic. The Carthaginians began to expand their influence from their coastal colonies northwards during the later 3rd Century BC. The Carthaginians and Romans eventually settled upon areas of mutual influence divided by the Ebro river, each supporting its allied cities and tribes within its own client territories. However, due to the ambitions of the Carthaginian Barca family this situation was bound not to last for long. In 219 BC a dispute broke out between the city of Saguntum and its neighbours who were part of the Punic protectorate. The Carthaginian general Hannibal Barca came to the rescue of Carthage's allies and attacked Saguntum which was itself allied to Rome. The Romans reacted with predictable outrage and demanded Hannibal be handed over to Rome for breaking their treaty. Understandably the Carthaginian oligarchy refused to surrender their general and the two great nations were drawn into the Second Punic War.

Spain was not entirely subdued until the defeat of the Cantabrians by Augustus. As with so many of Rome's enemies, we have the Romans themselves to thank for descriptions of troops and fighting methods to provide the basis for a list. The names given, scutarii and caetrati, will therefore be familiar to anyone who has read their Livy. Admittedly, they would not have meant much to the native Spaniards though. The Romans obviously thought reasonably highly of Spanish skill at arms. The Roman pilum has its parallel in heavy javelins used by the Spanish, including a version supposedly made entirely of iron. The Roman military sword of the imperial era is known as the 'Spanish' sword – the *gladius hispaniensis*. The north and centre of Spain was occupied by Celtic tribes called Celtiberians. These are represented in the list as warbands along the same lines as Gauls and other Celts, and note that there is a separate list covering the Celtiberians.

Search: The Punic Wars, The Numantine War, Lusitania, the Cantabrian War.

Infantry 75%+	At least three quarters of the units in the army must be infantry other than skirmishers.
Scutarii at least 25% of infantry units	At least a quarter of the non-skirmisher infantry units in the army must be scutarii.
Cavalry up to 25%	Up to a quarter of the units in the army can be cavalry.
Divisions 4+ units	Divisions must contain at least 4 units excluding skirmishers and must be led by a commander. If the general's guard is fielded it must form part of the general's division.
Skirmishers per division 50% of infantry	Divisions may contain up to half as many skirmisher units as they contain non-skirmisher infantry.

Spanish Troop Values

Unit	Clash	Sustained	Short Range	Long Range	Morale Save	Stamina	Special	Points Value
Scutarii medium infantry armed with throwing spears	6	6	3	0	5+	6		23 per unit
• *Extra to give scutarii heavy javelins counting as pila*	6	6	3	0	5+	6		+3 per unit
• *Extra to upgrade scutarii to general's guard – up to 1 unit*	7	7	3	0	5+	6	Fanatic, Tough fighters	+4 per unit
Caetrati light infantry with javelins and fielded as small units	3	3	2	0	0	4		12 per unit
Celtiberian medium infantry warbands armed with sword and javelins	8	6	2	0	5+	6	Wild fighters	27 per unit
Skirmishers with javelins fielded as small units	3	2	2	0	0	4		11 per unit
Skirmishers with slings fielded as small units	2	2	2	2	0	4		12 per unit
• *Extra to make slingers marksmen*	2	2	2	2	0	4	Marksmen	+1 per unit
Medium cavalry armed with spears/javelins	8	5	3	0	5+	6	Tough fighters	28 per unit
Caetrati light infantry fielded as small units – up to 1 per medium cavalry unit	3	3	2	0	0	4	Sub-unit of cavalry	12 per unit
Light cavalry armed with javelins and fielded as small units	5	3	2	0	6+	4		17 per unit
Commanders			1 commander must be provided per division. All commanders including general have leadership 8.					Free

This list represents the Macedonian successors to Alexander the Great. They were known as the Antigonids, being the descendants of Antigonus Monopthalmus (the One-Eyed). The Macedonians fought a series of wars against the Romans which the Romans eventually won by dint of their greater numbers and limitless resources rather than their military superiority. The Battle of Pydna in 167 BC resulted in the defeat of the Macedonians and paved the way for Roman expansion into the Hellenistic world.

Search: The Antigonids, Battle of Pydna, Battle of Cynoscephalae.

Infantry 25%+	At least a quarter of the units in the army must be infantry other than skirmishers.
Pike 25%+ of infantry	At least a quarter of the non-skirmisher infantry units in the army must be pike-armed phalanx of one type or another.
Cavalry 25%+	At least a quarter of the units in the army must be cavalry.
Artillery up to 1	Up to one unit of artillery can be included in the army.
Divisions 4+ units	Divisions must contain at least 4 units excluding skirmishers and must be led by a commander.
Skirmishers per division 50% of infantry	Divisions may contain up to half as many skirmisher units as they contain non-skirmisher infantry.

Late Macedonian Troop Values

Unit	Clash	Sustained	Short Range	Long Range	Morale Save	Stamina	Special	Points Value
Phalangite heavy infantry armed with pikes	7	7	3/0	0	4+	6	Phalanx	32 per unit
• Extra to upgrade phalangites to veteran – up to half	7	7	3/0	0	4+	6	Phalanx, Drilled	+3 per unit
• Extra to upgrade phalangites to guard – up to 1 unit	7	7	3/0	0	4+	6	Phalanx, Drilled, Elite	+6 per unit
Thureophoroi, Illyrian or Thracian light infantry with spears and/or javelins	5	5	3	0	6+	6		20 per unit
• Reduction to field Thracians or Illyrians with javelins as small units	3	3	2	0	6+	4		–7 per unit
• Extra to field standard size Thracians with double-handed rhomphaia – up to 1 unit	6	5	2/0	0	6+	6	Tough fighter	+2 per unit
• Extra to upgrade Thureophoroi to Thorakitai medium infantry	6	6	3	0	5+	6		+3 per unit
Galatian medium infantry warband with swords and javelins – up to 1 unit	9	6	2	0	5+	6	Wild fighters	28 per unit
• Extra to field Galatians as naked fanatics	9	6	2	0	5+	6	Wild fighters, Fanatic, Frenzied charge	+4 per unit
Skirmishers armed with javelins and fielded as small units	3	2	2	0	0	4		11 per unit
Cretan skirmishers with bows fielded as a small unit – up to 1 unit	2	2	2	2	0	4	Marksmen	13 per unit
Macedonian, Thracian or Thessalian medium cavalry armed with spears and/or javelins	8	5	3	0	5+	6	Drilled	30 per unit
• Extra to upgrade Macedonian cavalry to guard – up to 1 unit	9	6	3	0	5+	6	Drilled, Elite	+5 per unit
Greek medium cavalry armed with spears and/or javelins	8	5	3	0	5+	6		27 per unit
Galatian medium cavalry armed with spears and/or javelins – up to 1 unit	8	5	3	0	5+	6	Tough fighters	28 per unit
Greek light cavalry armed with javelins and fielded as small units	5	3	2	0	6+	4		17 per unit
• Extra to field Greek light cavalry as Illyrians	5	3	2	0	6+	4	Feigned flight	+2 per unit
Medium artillery bolt thrower – up to 1 unit	1	1	0	3	0	3		20 per unit
Commanders		1 commander must be provided per division. All commanders including general have leadership 8						Free

Seleucus emerged from the civil wars that followed Alexander the Great's death as the master of much of the old Persian empire. The dynasty that he founded is known as the Seleucid dynasty, and the Seleucid empire lasted in some form or other until the annexation of Syria by the Romans. This list represents the armies of the empire before the rot set in, when the Seleucids could still give the Romans a good run for their money and contend for the hegemony of the Hellenistic East. Although originally based upon Babylonia, the centre of the Seleucid empire gradually shifted to Syria and its capital of Antioch – just one of many cities so-named by Seleucus to honour his father Antiochus, who was a general of Alexander's father Philip. At its height the Seleucid Empire stretched as far east as India, to Sogdia in the north east, to the borders of Egypt in the south and westward as far as the Aegean.

Search: Antiochus III, The Battle of Ispus (301 BC), The Syrian Wars, The Battle of Raphia, The Roman-Syrian War, The Battle of Magnesia.

Infantry 25%+	At least a quarter of the units in the army must be infantry other than skirmishers.
Pike 25%+ of infantry	At least a quarter of the non-skirmisher infantry units in the army must be pike-armed phalanx of one type or another.
Cavalry 25%+	At least a quarter of the units in the army must be cavalry.
Artillery up to 3	Up to one unit of each type can be included and no more than one in ten of the number of units in the army in total.
Heavy scythed chariots up to 3	The army can include up to 3 heavy scythed chariots.
Elephants up to 10%	Up to one in ten units in the army can be elephants.
Divisions 4+ units	Divisions must contain at least 4 units excluding skirmishers and must be led by a commander.
Skirmishers per division 50% of infantry	Divisions may contain up to half as many skirmisher units as they contain non-skirmisher infantry.

Seleucid Troop Values

Unit	Clash	Sustained	Short Range	Long Range	Morale Save	Stamina	Special	Points Value
Phalangite heavy infantry armed with pikes	7	7	3/0	0	4+	6	Phalanx	32 per unit
• *Extra to upgrade phalangite to veteran – up to half*	7	7	3/0	0	4+	6	*Phalanx, Drilled*	*+3 per unit*
• *Extra to upgrade phalangite to guard – up to 1 unit*	7	7	3/0	0	4+	6	*Phalanx, Drilled, Elite, Stubborn*	*+9 per unit*
Light infantry peltasts with spears/javelins	5	5	3	0	6+	6		20 per unit
• *Extra to field light infantry as Thracians with double-handed rhomphaia – up to 1 unit*	6	5	2/0	0	6+	6	*Tough fighter*	*+2 per unit*
• *Reduction to field javelin-armed peltasts as small unit*	3	3	2	0	6+	4		*–7 per unit*
Thorakitai medium infantry with spears and javelins	6	6	3	0	5+	6		23 per unit
Cappodacian light infantry with javelins fielded as small units	3	3	2	0	6+	4		13 per unit
Galatian medium infantry warband with swords and javelins – up to 1 unit	9	6	2	0	5+	6	Wild fighters	28 per unit
• *Extra to field Galatian warband as naked fanatics*	9	6	2	0	5+	6	*Wild fighters, Fanatic, Frenzied charge*	*+4 per unit*
Skirmishers armed with javelins and fielded as small units	3	2	2	0	0	4		11 per unit
• *Extra to give skirmishers slings instead of javelins – up to half*	2	2	2	2	0	4		*+1 per unit*
• *Extra to give skirmishers bows instead of javelins – up to half*	2	2	2	2	0	4		*+1 per unit*
○ *Extra to upgrade skirmisher bowmen to Cretans*	2	2	2	2	0	4	*Marksmen*	*+1 per unit*
• *Reduction to make any above skirmishers other than Cretans levy – up to half*			——— *As above* ———				*Levy*	*–2 per unit*

Seleucid Troop Values

Unit	Clash	Sustained	Short Range	Long Range	Morale Save	Stamina	Special	Points Value
Agema heavy cavalry armed with spears	9	6	3	0	4+	6	Drilled, Elite	36 per unit
• Extra to upgrade Agema to cataphracts	9	6	3	0	4+	6	Drilled, Elite	+1 per unit
• Extra to give any of the above Agema kontos	9	6	3/0	0	4+	6	Drilled, Elite	+3 per unit
Line medium cavalry armed with spears	8	5	3	0	5+	6	Drilled	30 per unit
• Extra to upgrade line cavalry to heavy cavalry	9	6	3	0	4+	6	Drilled	+3 per unit
• Extra to upgrade line cavalry to cataphracts	9	6	3	0	4+	6	Drilled	+4 per unit
• Extra to give any of the above kontos			— As above —				Drilled	+3 per unit
Civic militia medium cavalry with javelins and/or spears – up to 1 unit	8	5	3	0	5+	6	Levy	24 per unit
Galatian medium cavalry armed with spears/javelins – up to 1 unit	8	5	3	0	5+	6	Tough fighters	28 per unit
Light cavalry armed with javelins and fielded as small units	5	3	2	0	6+	4		17 per unit
• Extra to give light cavalry feigned flight	5	3	2	0	6+	4	Feigned flight	+2 per unit
Horse archers fielded as a small unit – up to 1 unit	4	2	2	2	6+	4	Parthian shot	19 per unit
Elephants with mixed armed crews	4	3	1	1	4+	6	Elephant	24 per unit
Light infantry elephant guard with slings and bows (range as slings) fielded as small units – up to 1 per elephant	3	3	2	2	0	4	Sub-unit of elephant	14 per unit
• Reduction to field light infantry elephant guard with javelins	3	3	2	0	0	4	Sub-unit of elephant	−2 per unit
Heavy scythed chariot fielded as 1 model	7	0	0	0	3+	4	Scythed chariot	10 per unit
Light artillery bolt throwers	1	1	2	2	0	3		15 per unit
Medium artillery bolt or stone throwers	1	1	0	3	0	3		20 per unit
Heavy artillery stone throwers	1	1	0	3	0	3		23 per unit
Commanders		1 commander must be provided per division. All commanders including general have leadership 8						Free

"War is the mother of everything."

Heraclitus

PTOLEMAIC

Mid 3rd–1st centuries BC

Following the break up of Alexander the Great's empire Ptolemy I emerged as the ruler of Egypt. The dynasty he founded was to last the longest of all of the Successors, ending only with the death of Cleopatra in 30 BC. The chief rival of the Ptolemies was the Seleucid empire to the north. The two Hellenistic kingdoms fought incessantly for control of the territory that lay between Egypt and Syria. Elephants were an important part of these opposing armies. The Ptolemies began with a herd of Indian elephants but, being unable to obtain replacements, attempted to train African elephants instead. These proved unsatisfactory, being the smaller elephants native to North Africa. In a confrontation between the two kinds of elephant the Indian beasts of the Seleucids had the advantage. To represent this, in any straightforward fight between the two kinds, the African elephants lose 1 hand-to-hand combat attack. I have not included contemporary Roman legionaries fighting on behalf of Cleopatra as we felt it was rather untypical of Ptolemaic armies up to that time – see the Marian Roman list for stats.

Search: Ptolemy I Soter, The Battle of Gaza (312 BC), Syrian Wars, The Battle of Raphia.

Infantry 25%+	At least a quarter of the units in the army must be infantry other than skirmishers.
Pike 25%+ of infantry	At least a quarter of the non-skirmisher infantry units in the army must be pike-armed phalanx of one type or another.
Cavalry 25%+	At least a quarter of the units in the army must be cavalry.
Artillery up to 1	Up to one unit.
Elephants up to 10%	Up to one in ten units in the army can be elephants.
Divisions 4+ units	Divisions must contain at least 4 units excluding skirmishers and be led by a commander.
Skirmishers per division 50% of infantry	Divisions may contain up to half as many skirmisher units as they contain non-skirmisher infantry.

Ptolemaic Troop Values

Unit	Clash	Sustained	Short Range	Long Range	Morale Save	Stamina	Special	Points Value
Phalangite heavy infantry armed with pikes	7	7	3/0	0	4+	6	Phalanx	32 per unit
• *Reduction to field phalangites as Egyptian levy*	6	6	3/0	0	4+	6	*Phalanx, Levy*	*−5 per unit*
• *Extra to upgrade phalangites to veteran – up to half*	7	7	3/0	0	4+	6	*Phalanx, Drilled*	*+3 per unit*
• *Extra to upgrade phalangites to guard – up to 1 unit*	7	7	3/0	0	4+	6	*Phalanx, Drilled, Elite, Stubborn*	*+9 per unit*
Light infantry peltasts with spears/javelins	5	5	3	0	6+	6		20 per unit
• *Extra to field peltasts as Thracians with double-handed rhomphaia – up to 1 unit*	6	5	2/0	0	6+	6	*Tough fighters*	*+2 per unit*
◦ *Reduction to field light javelin-armed peltasts as small units*	3	3	2	0	6+	4		*−7 per unit*
Galatian medium infantry warband with swords and javelins – up to 1 unit	9	6	2	0	5+	6	Wild fighters	28 per unit
• *Extra to field Galatians as naked fanatics*	9	6	2	0	5+	6	*Wild fighters, Fanatic, Frenzied charge*	*+4 per unit*
Skirmishers armed with javelins and fielded as small units	3	2	2	0	0	4		11 per unit
• *Extra to field skirmishers as Aetolian – up to 1 unit*	2	2	2	0	0	4	*Marksmen*	*+1 per unit*
Egyptian, Arab or Jewish skirmishers armed with slings fielded as small units	2	2	2	2	0	4	Levy	10 per unit
Egyptian or Syrian or Arab skirmishers armed with bows and fielded as small units	2	2	2	2	0	4	Levy	10 per unit
• *Extra to upgrade bowmen to Cretans – up to 1 unit*	2	2	2	2	0	4	*Marksmen*	*+3 per unit*
Agema heavy cavalry armed with spears and/or javelins	9	6	3	0	4+	6	Drilled, Elite	36 per unit
Cleruch medium cavalry armed with spears and/or javelins	8	5	3	0	5+	6	Drilled	30 per unit
Light cavalry armed with javelins and fielded as small units	5	3	2	0	6+	4		17 per unit
• *Extra to give light cavalry feigned flight*	5	3	2	0	6+	4	*Feigned flight*	*+2 per unit*
Arab camel-mounted light cavalry with bows and javelins fielded as a small unit – up to 1 unit	4	3	2	2	6+	4	Feigned flight	20 per unit
Elephants with mixed armed crews	4	3	1	1	4+	6	Elephant	24 per unit
Libyan four-horse light chariots with javelin-armed crews	8	6	3	0	4+	6		29 per unit
Medium artillery bolt thrower – up to 1 unit	1	1	0	3	0	3		20 per unit
Commanders		1 commander must be provided per division. All commanders including general have leadership 8						Free

The Han dynasty corresponds in time to the rise and height of Roman power in the west beginning in 206 BC and ending in 220 AD. This was a period of great progress for China. Contacts were made with the other great empires of the ancient world in Parthia and even Rome. This list owes something to its immediate predecessor the Qin army, with a new emphasis on the mounted arm. Light cavalry with crossbows can be treated as bow-armed, this type of Chinese crossbow being very light and suitable for use on horseback. Chinese archers can be armed with bows or crossbows; a weapon that the Chinese perfected and produced in many variants of size and weight. Troops armed with repeating type crossbows – a uniquely Chinese weapon – are treated as bow armed in all respects, whilst heavier crossbows can be treated as bows or as crossbows as preferred. Chariots went out of use as weapons of war during the Han dynasty, ceasing to form part of Chinese armies during the Western Han (ie, by 9 AD). Chinese chariots are classed as light chariots and appear to have been relatively lightly built and mobile. The option to field troops as rebel militia allows the army to represent insurrectionist forces. Some of these became established as the personal forces of Han generals towards the end of the dynasty.

Search: Lui Bang, The Battle of Baideng, Rebellion of the Seven States, The Yellow Turban Rebellion, Battle of Red Cliffs.

Infantry 25%+	At least a quarter of the units in the army must be infantry other than skirmishers.
Cavalry 25%+	At least a quarter of the units in the army must be cavalry.
Chariots up to 10%	Up to one in ten units in the army can be chariots.
Artillery up to 3 units	The army can include up to 3 units of artillery.
Divisions 4+ units	Divisions must contain at least 4 units excluding skirmishers and must be led by a commander. Southern tribal troops – where present – must form their own division/divisions, which may include skirmishers as noted below.
Skirmishers per division 50% of infantry	Divisions may contain up to half as many skirmisher units as they contain non-skirmisher infantry.

Han China Troop Values

Unit	Clash	Sustained	Short Range	Long Range	Morale Save	Stamina	Special	Points Value
Heavy infantry armed with spears and swords	7	7	3	0	4+	6	Drilled	29 per unit
• Extra to upgrade heavy infantry to veteran – up to half	7	7	3	0	4+	6	Drilled, Elite	+3 per unit
• Extra to incorporate archers into the rear ranks of any of the above	7	7	3	2	4+	6	As above	+2 per unit
• Extra to give any of the above heavy infantry and/or veterans long spears	7	7	3/0	As above	4+	6	As above	+3 per unit
Medium infantry armed with spears and swords	6	6	3	0	5+	6	Drilled	26 per unit
• Extra to incorporate archers into rear ranks	6	6	3	2	5+	6	Drilled	+2 per unit
• Reduction to field any of the above as impressed convicts or rebel militia	——————— As above ———————						Levy	–6 per unit
° Extra to make rebel militia fanatic	——————— As above ———————						Levy, Fanatic	+1 per unit
Light infantry swordsmen	5	5	3	0	6+	6		20 per unit
• Extra to make swordsmen elite with sword in both hands – up to 1 unit	6	6	3	0	6+	6	Elite, Tough fighters	+6 per unit
• Extra to give swordmen double-handed swords – up to 1 unit	6	5	2/0	0	6+	6	Tough fighters	+2 per unit
Light infantry archers with bows or crossbows	4	4	3	3	6+	6		21 per unit
• Reduction to field light infantry archers as small units	3	3	2	2	6+	4		–6 per unit
Southern tribal medium infantry warbands with spears and/or javelins	8	6	2	0	5+	6		24 per unit
Southern tribal light infantry archers fielded as small units	3	3	2	2	0	4		14 per unit
Skirmishers armed with javelins and fielded as small units	3	2	2	0	0	4		11 per unit

The Celtiberians were Celtic tribes settled in Spain. They took part in the wars between Carthage and Rome and continued to resist the Romans on their own afterwards. During the Second Punic War numerous Celtiberians cross Italy as part of Hannibal's army. The Lusitanians, who lived in what is roughly speaking modern Portugal, were famous for their hit-and-run style of warfare. They were masters of the stealthy ambush, and are here represented by light infantry with the marauder rule. Note that I have separated out the Celtiberians from the Spanish armies to more easily represent the wars in Spain that followed the end of the Punic Wars. For example, the Numantine Wars of 154 BC-13 BC. Players who wish to combine both lists can certainly do so where history suggests it.

Search: The Punic Wars, The Celtiberian Wars, Numantia, The Sertorian War.

Infantry 75%+	At least three quarters of the units in the army must be infantry other than skirmishers.
Warbands or Lusitanians 50%+ of infantry	Either warbands or Lusitanians must make up at least a half of the non-skirmisher infantry units in the army – representing either a Celtiberian or specifically Lusitanian army.
Cavalry up to 25%	Up to a quarter of the units in the army can be cavalry.
Divisions 4+ units	Divisions must contain at least 4 units other than skirmishers and be led by a commander. If general's guard is fielded these must form part of the general's division.
Skirmishers per division 50% of infantry	Divisions may contain up to half as many skirmisher units as they contain non-skirmisher infantry.

Celtiberian Troop Values

Unit	Combat				Morale Save	Stamina	Special	Points Value
	Clash	Sustained	Short Range	Long Range				
Celtiberian medium infantry warband armed with sword and javelins	8	6	2	0	5+	6		24 per unit
• Extra to make warbands 'wild fighters'	8	6	2	0	5+	6	Wild fighters	+3 per unit
Celiberian medium infantry bodyguard warband – up to 1 unit	8	6	2	0	5+	6	Tough fighters, Fanatic, Valiant	29 per unit
Lusitanian light infantry armed with javelins and/or spears	5	5	3	0	6+	6	Marauders	23 per unit
Skirmishers with javelins fielded as small units	3	2	2	0	0	4		11 per unit
• Extra to field skirmishers with slings – up to half	2	2	2	2	0	4		+1 per unit
Medium cavalry armed with spears and/or javelins	8	5	3	0	5+	6		27 per unit
Light infantry armed with spears and/or javelins fielded as small units – up to 1 per cavalry	3	3	2	0	0	4	Sub-unit of cavalry	12 per unit
Light cavalry armed with javelins and fielded as small units	5	3	2	0	6+	4		17 per unit
Commanders	—	1 commander must be provided per division All commanders including general have leadership 8						Free

CAESAR'S GALLIC WARS

Caesar tells us that Gaul is divided into three parts: inhabited by the Belgae, the Aquitani and the Gauls. He also says these differ from each other in language, customs and laws. Of all these he says, the Belgae are the bravest, being the furthest from civilization, and being the nearest to the Germans with whom they are continually waging war. Of the Gauls, Caesar considers the Helvetii greatest in valor, as they contend with the Germans in almost daily battles, when they either repel them from their own territories, or themselves wage war on their frontiers.

'Duck-bill' axe head
Middle Kingdom c.19th Century BC
(Perry Collection)

Pyrrhus of Epirus was one of the greatest generals of his age – it was in his blood – after all he was second cousin to Alexander the Great. He became King of Epirus and Macedonia and led armies against the Romans in support of the Greek cities of southern Italy (known as Magna Graecia). The victories he won during that campaign were achieved at such cost to his own army the term 'pyrrhic victory' passed into common usage to describe a victory almost as crippling to the winners as the losers. The Epirote army is typical of the western Successors in that it is based upon the pike-armed phalanx supported by lighter infantry and cavalry. We have represented the Macedonian and Epirote cavalry as armed with light spears, which seems more in keeping with the general effectiveness of Greek cavalry following the days of Alexander. The proportion of pikes in Pyrrhus's armies fell in succeeding battles. The proportions described already allow for this and players wishing to model the earliest battles will no doubt wish to field more than the minimum indicated.

Search: Pyrrhus of Epirus, The Battle of Heraclea (280 BC), The Battle of Asculum (279 BC), The Battle of Beneventum (275 BC).

Infantry 50%+	At least half the units in the army must be infantry other than skirmishers.
Pike 25%+ of infantry	At least a quarter of the non-skirmisher infantry units in the army must be pike-armed phalanx of one type or another.
Cavalry up to 50%	Up to half of the units in the army can be cavalry.
Artillery up to 1	The army can include up to one unit of artillery.
Elephants up to 10%	Up to one in ten units in the army can be elephants.
Divisions 4+ units	Divisions must contain at least 4 units excluding skirmishers and must be led by a commander.
Skirmishers per division 50% of infantry	Divisions may contain up to half as many skirmisher units as they contain non-skirmisher infantry.

Pyrrhic Troop Values

Unit	Clash	Sustained	Short Range	Long Range	Morale Save	Stamina	Special	Points Value
Phalangite heavy infantry armed with pikes	7	7	3/0	0	4+	6	Phalanx	32 per unit
• Extra to upgrade phalangite to veteran – up to half	7	7	3/0	0	4+	6	Phalanx, Drilled	+3 per unit
• Reduction to field phalangite as raw Tarentines	7	7	3/0	0	4+	6	Phalanx, Levy	–3 per unit
Greek, Italian or Oscan hoplite heavy infantry armed with long spears	7	7	3/0	0	4+	6	Phalanx	32 per unit
Oscan light infantry with spears/javelins	5	5	3	0	6+	6		20 per unit
Galatian medium infantry warbands armed with swords and javelins	9	6	2	0	5+	6	Wild fighters	28 per unit
Oscan light infantry with spears/javelins	5	5	3	0	6+	6		20 per unit
Skirmishers armed with javelins and fielded as small units	3	2	2	0	0	4		11 per unit
Skirmishers armed with slings and fielded as small units	2	2	2	2	0	4		12 per unit
Skirmishers armed with bows and fielded as small units	2	2	2	2	0	4		12 per unit
• Extra to upgrade bowmen to Cretans	2	2	2	2	0	4	Marksmen	+1 per unit
Epirote or Macedonian medium cavalry with spears and/or javelins	8	5	3	0	5+	6	Drilled, Elite	33 per unit
• Extra to upgrade Epirote or Macedonians to heavy cavalry	9	6	3	0	4+	6	Drilled, Elite	+3 per unit
Allied Thessalian or Greek medium cavalry armed with spears and/or javelins	8	5	3	0	5+	6	Drilled	30 per unit
Oscan medium cavalry armed with spears and/or javelins	8	5	3	0	5+	6	Elite	30 per unit
• Extra to upgrade Oscan cavalry to heavy cavalry	9	6	3	0	4+	6	Elite	+3 per unit

Unit	Combat				Morale Save	Stamina	Special	Points Value
	Clash	Sustained	Short Range	Long Range				
Light cavalry armed with javelins and fielded as small units	5	3	2	0	6+	4		17 per unit
• Extra to make light cavalry Tarentines	5	3	2	0	6+	4	Feigned flight	+2 per unit
Elephants with javelin-armed crews	4	3	1	0	4+	6	Elephant	23 per unit
Medium artillery bolt thrower – up to 1 unit	1	1	0	3	0	3		20 per unit
Commanders	1 commander must be provided per division. All commanders including general have leadership 8							Free
Extra to upgrade general to leadership 9	The general can have leadership 9 at the following extra cost							+25

EARLY GERMAN

Germans fought in a style comparable to the Gauls, represented here as warbands armed with a mix of spears, javelins and swords. The Chatti are sometimes assumed to carry longer spears. I take the view that these were used in a general way and not in the fashion of Greek hoplites. Those who think otherwise may field warbands with long spears at +3 pts per unit and 0/2 short-range attacks. I have suggested upgrades for eager and brave units. This allows for some characterisation of tribes and distinguishes the Germans from their Dacian, British and Gallic cousins. Cavalry and infantry sometimes fought intermixed. To represent this any unit of light cavalry can be combined with one small unit of skirmishers with both treated as sub-units of the other. So long as infantry remain within 6" of their cavalry whilst both move their move rate is increased to 9". If a general's guard unit is fielded it must be part of the general's division.

Search: Cimbri, Teutones, Cherusci, Chatti, Suevi, Chauci, Battle of the Teutoberg Forest, Arminius, Marcomannic Wars, Quadi, Buri.

Infantry 75%+	At least three quarters of the units in the army must be infantry other than skirmishers.
Warbands 50%+ of infantry	At least half the non-skirmisher infantry units in the army must be medium infantry warbands.
Divisions 4+ units	Divisions must contain at least 4 units excluding skirmishers and must be led by a commander. If a general's guard unit is fielded it must be part of the general's division.
Skirmishers per division 50% of infantry	Divisions may contain up to half as many skirmisher units as they contain non-skirmisher infantry.

Early German Troop Values								
Unit	**Combat**				**Morale Save**	**Stamina**	**Special**	**Points Value**
	Clash	Sustained	Short Range	Long Range				
Medium infantry warbands armed with javelins or spears	9	6	2	0	5+	6	Wild fighters	28 per unit
• Extra to field warbands as brave	9	6	2	0	5+	6	Wild fighters, Brave	+3 per unit
• Extra to field a warband as general's guard – up to 1 unit	9	6	2	0	5+	6	Brave, Wild fighters, Stubborn	+5 per unit
• Extra to field a warband as eager – up to 1 unit	9	6	2	0	5+	6	Eager, Wild fighters,	Free
Light infantry archers	4	4	3	3	0	6		20 per unit
• Reduction to field archers as small units	3	3	2	2	0	4		–6 per unit
Skirmishers with javelins fielded as small units	3	2	2	0	0	4		11 per unit
• Extra to give skirmishers bows – up to 1 unit	2	2	2	2	0	4		+1 per unit
Light cavalry armed with javelins and fielded as small units	5	3	2	0	6+	4		17 per unit
Medium cavalry armed with spears and javelins	8	5	3	0	5+	6	Eager, Tough fighters	28 per unit
Commanders	1 commander must be provided per division. All commanders including general have leadership 8.							Free

The Maccabeans started out as a rag-tag alliance of bandits and rebels fighting a guerrilla war from the hills, raiding and ambushing the Seleucid controlled garrisons and towns. As they used captured equipment their appearance would have been comparable that of other Hellenistic warriors of the day. The spearmen, different types of skirmishers and cavalry are drawn from the Dead Sea Scrolls description of the Jewish army. The option to ditch the spearmen and field an army based on zealots allows for the earliest phases of the revolt. Zealots would have been variously armed with whatever came to hand, so potentially the same figures can be used to make up both troop types.

Search: Judah Maccabee, Books 1 & 2 Maccabees of the Apocrypha, War of the Sons of Light Against the Sons of Darkness.

Cavalry up to 25%	Up to a quarter of the units in the army can be cavalry.
Light cavalry 50%+ of cavalry	At least half the cavalry units in the army must be light cavalry.
Medium infantry OR zealots 50%+ of infantry	At least half the non-skirmisher infantry units must be either medium infantry OR if the army has no medium infantry at all, at least half the infantry must be zealots instead. A medium infantry based army can include zealots – but in smaller numbers.
Divisions 4+ units	Divisions must contain at least 4 units excluding skirmishers and must be led by a commander.
Skirmishers per division 50% of infantry	Divisions may contain up to half as many skirmisher units as they contain non-skirmisher infantry.

Maccabean Jewish Troop Values

Unit	Clash	Sustained	Short Range	Long Range	Morale Save	Stamina	Special	Points Value
Medium infantry with spears and/or javelins	6	6	3	0	5+	6		23 per unit
• Reduction to make medium infantry freshly raised	6	6	3	0	5+	6	Freshly raised	–1 per unit
Medium infantry with long spears and javelins	6	6	3	0	5+	6		26 per unit
• Extra to make medium infantry with long spears phalanx	6	6	3/0	0	5+	6	Phalanx	+3 per unit
Zealot light Infantry with javelins	5	5	3	0	6+	6	Wild fighters, Frenzied charge	26 per unit
Light infantry with bows	4	4	3	3	0	6		20 per unit
Skirmishers with javelins fielded as small units	3	2	2	0	0	4		11 per unit
Skirmishers with slings fielded as small units	2	2	2	2	0	4		12 per unit
Skirmishers with bows fielded as a small unit – up to 1 unit	2	2	2	2	0	4		12 per unit
Medium cavalry armed with spears and/or javelins	8	5	3	0	5+	6		27 per unit
Medium cavalry armed with kontos	8	5	3/0	0	5+	6		30 per unit
Heavy cavalry armed with spears and/or javelins	9	6	3	0	4+	6		30 per unit
Heavy cavalry armed with kontos	9	6	3/0	0	4+	6		33 per unit
Cataphract cavalry armed with kontos – up to 1 unit	9	6	3/0	0	4+	6		34 per unit
Light cavalry armed with javelins and fielded as small units	5	3	2	0	6+	4		17 per unit
Light cavalry armed with javelins and bows and fielded as small units	5	3	2	2	6+	4		19 per unit
Commanders	1 commander must be provided per division. All commanders including general have leadership 8.							Free

"A tomb now suffices him for whom the world was not enough."

Epitaph upon Alexander the Great

SARMATIANS

The Sarmatians were a group of western Scythians who settled north of the Danube where they appear to have rubbed shoulders with the Dacians. They fought as heavy cavalry and are famously depicted on Trajan's Column covered from head to toe in scale armour, and riding horses similarly protected. All Sarmatian cavalry carried bows but were notorious for ignoring them and charging hell for leather at the first opportunity. For this reason their long range shooting has been downgraded. Medium cavalry represent less well-equipped riders, but could also be Alans. The Alans were a neighbouring or subject tribe who preferred to fight in this way. Similarly, light cavalry could represent younger, low-status individuals serving as scouts and flank guards or similarly equipped Alans in looser formation. An Alanic army, as opposed to Iazyges or Roxolani for example, could conceivably forego heavy cavalry and infantry altogether, leaving an army entirely composed of medium and light cavalry.

Search: Iazyges, Roxolani, Alani, Siraces, Dacian Wars.

Cavalry 75%+	At least three quarters of the units in the army must be cavalry.
Heavy cavalry/cataphracts 50%+ of cavalry	At least half the cavalry units in the army must be heavy cavalry or cataphracts.
Infantry up to 25%	Up to a quarter of the unit in the army can be infantry other than skirmishers.
Divisions 4+ units	Divisions must contain at least 4 units excluding skirmishers and must be led by a commander.
Skirmishers per division 50% of infantry	Divisions may contain up to half as many skirmisher units as they contain non-skirmisher infantry.

Sarmatian Troop Values

Unit	Clash	Sustained	Short Range	Long Range	Morale Save	Stamina	Special	Points Value
Heavy cavalry with kontos and bows	9	6	3	1	4+	6		34 per unit
• *Upgrade heavy cavalry to cataphracts*	9	6	3	1	4+	6		*+1 per unit*
• *Make heavy or cataphract cavalry eager*	9	6	3	1	4+	6	*Eager*	*Free*
• *Give any of the above frenzied charge*	9	6	3	1	4+	6	*As above + Frenzied charge*	*+3 per unit*
Medium cavalry with spear and/or javelins and bows	8	5	3	2	5+	6		29 per unit
• *Make medium cavalry eager*	8	5	3	2	5+	6	*Eager*	*Free*
• *Give any of the above frenzied charge*	8	5	3	2	5+	6	*As above +Frenzied charge*	*+3 per unit*
Light cavalry armed with bows and javelins and fielded as small units	5	3	2	2	6+	4		19 per unit
Subject levy spearmen – medium infantry with spears and/or javelins	6	6	3	0	5+	6	Levy	20 per unit
Subject levy medium infantry archers – up to 1 per subject spearman unit	5	5	3	3	5+	6	Levy	21 per unit
• *Reduction to field levy archers as light infantry – up to half*	4	4	3	3	0	6	*Levy*	*–4 per unit*
◦ *Reduction to field light infantry archers as small units*	3	3	2	2	0	4	*Levy*	*–5 per unit*
Skirmishers with javelins fielded as a small unit – up to 1 unit	3	2	2	0	0	4		11 per unit
Commanders			1 commander must be provided per division All commanders including general have leadership 8					Free

This army hails from the brief Armenian Empire that spread over much of the disintegrating Seleucid domains and can therefore include a number of subject peoples from the adjoining regions. Cataphract and heavy cavalry can be from Armenia, Gordyene, Adiabene, Media Atropatene and adjoining regions of the Parthian empire as well as Syria. Lighter cavalry come from the same areas plus Cappadocia, Cilicia and Commagene to the west and Iberia and Albania to the north. The same areas would provide the infantry, who might therefore have the same general appearance as Parthian or Hellenised troops. The phalangites are former Seleucid troops and the imitation legionaries a deliberate, and largely unsuccessful, attempt to train troops to face the Romans.

Search: Tigranes the Great, Battle of Tigranocerta.

Cavalry 25%+	At least a quarter of the units in the army must be cavalry.
Infantry 25%+	At least a quarter of the units in the army must be infantry other than skirmishers.
Divisions 4+ units	Divisions must contain at least 4 units excluding skirmishers and must be led by a commander.
Skirmishers per division 50% of infantry	Divisions may contain up to half as many skirmisher units as they contain non-skirmisher infantry.

Artaxiad Armenian Troop Values

Unit	Clash	Sustained	Short Range	Long Range	Morale Save	Stamina	Special	Points Value
Cataphract cavalry armed with kontos	9	6	3/0	0	4+	6		34 per unit
Heavy cavalry armed with kontos	9	6	3/0	0	4+	6		33 per unit
Horse archers fielded as small units	4	2	2	2	6+	4	Parthian shot	19 per unit
Light cavalry armed with javelins fielded as small units	5	3	2	0	6+	4	Feigned flight	19 per unit
Arab camel-mounted light cavalry with bows and javelins fielded as a small unit – up to 1 unit	4	3	2	2	6+	4	Feigned flight	20 per unit
Imitation Roman legionary heavy infantry armed with spears and/or javelins	6	6	3	0	4+	6		24 per unit
Phalangite heavy infantry armed with pikes	7	7	3/0	0	4+	6	Phalanx	32 per unit
Light infantry levy of armed servants with mixed weapons – up to 1 unit	4	4	2	0	6+	6	Levy, Wavering	7 per unit
Armenian or subject medium infantry armed with spears	6	6	3	0	5+	6		23 per unit
Armenian or subject medium infantry archers	5	5	3	3	5+	6		24 per unit
Armenian light infantry with spears and/or javelins	5	5	3	0	6+	6		20 per unit
Armenian light infantry archers	4	4	3	3	0	6		20 per unit
• *Reduction to field archers as small units*	3	3	2	2	0	4		–6 *per unit*
Skirmishers with javelins fielded as small units	3	2	2	0	0	4		11 per unit
Skirmishers with bows or slings fielded as small units	2	2	2	2	0	4		12 per unit
Commanders		1 commander must be provided per division						Free
		All commanders including general have leadership 8						

> "The victor is not victorious if the vanquished does not consider himself so."
>
> Quintus Ennius

This army represents the native forces that opposed Julius Caesar and whose descendants went on to resist the Claudian invasion and subsequent conquest of Britain. As such it is the army of Caratacus and Boudicca of the Iceni. The Britons fought much in the same fashion as their neighbours the Gauls, except that British cavalry seem to have been in short supply, with the role of the mounted arm fulfilled to some extent by light pony-drawn chariots. The mass of British warriors are represented as warbands with the usual mixture of javelins, spears and swords. I have made allowance for fielding cavalry as medium cavalry which may be a little generous but makes the army more varied and interesting as does the inclusion of bowmen. The British made great use of slings and piles of slingshot were found ready to use during the excavations of the hill fort at Maiden Castle which fell to the Romans during the initial phase of their invasion.

Search: Caratacus, Boadicea, Boudicca, The Battle of Watling Street, The Battle of the Medway.

Cavalry and/or chariots up to 50%	Up to half of the units in the army can be cavalry and/or chariots.
Infantry 50%+	At least half the units in the army must be made up of infantry other than skirmishers.
Warbands 50%+ of infantry	At least half the non-skirmisher infantry units in the army must comprise medium infantry warbands.
Divisions 4+ units	Divisions must contain at least 4 units excluding skirmishers and must be led by a commander.
Skirmishers per division 50% of infantry	Divisions may contain up to half as many skirmisher units as they contain non-skirmisher infantry.

Ancient British Troop Values

Unit	Combat				Morale Save	Stamina	Special	Points Value
	Clash	Sustained	Short Range	Long Range				
Medium infantry warband armed with swords and javelins	9	6	2	0	5+	6	Wild fighters	28 per unit
• *Extra to field warbands as large units*	*11*	*8*	*3*	*0*	*5+*	*8*	*Wild fighters*	*+7 per unit*
• *Extra to field one standard-sized warband as naked fanatics – up to 1 unit*	*9*	*6*	*2*	*0*	*5+*	*6*	*Wild fighters, Fanatic, Frenzied charge*	*+4 per unit*
Skirmishers with javelins fielded as small units	3	2	2	0	0	4		11 per unit
Skirmishers with slings fielded as small units	2	2	2	2	0	4		12 per unit
Skirmishers with bows fielded as a small unit – up to 1 unit	2	2	2	2	0	4		12 per unit
Medium cavalry armed with spears and/or javelins – up to 1 unit	8	5	3	0	5+	6		27 per unit
Light cavalry armed with javelins	7	5	3	0	6+	6		25 per unit
Light cavalry armed with javelins and fielded as small units	5	3	2	0	6+	4		17 per unit
British light chariots with crews armed with spears and javelins	6	5	4	0	4+	6		27 per unit
Commanders		1 commander must be provided per division						Free
		All commanders including general have leadership 8						

Pontus was a minor Successor kingdom that lay on the southern coast of the Black Sea in what is today Turkey. It reached its greatest height under Mithridates VI, also known as Mithridates the Great, in the first half of the first century BC. This is an army that shows the transition between the old Hellenistic phalanx and the Roman legionary – I have included both types in the list – over this period the phalangites were replaced by imitation legionaries and mercenary troops. Light cavalry and skirmishers could be from any of the territories occupied by the Pontic empire such as Cappadocia, Galatea, Lesser Armenia, Bithynia and Colchis. This makes quite an exotic army.

Search: Mithridates, The Asiatic Vespers, Battle of Chaeronea (86 BC), Battle of Zela (47 BC).

Cavalry 25%+	At least a quarter of the units in the army must be cavalry.
Infantry 25%+	At least a quarter of the units in the army must be infantry other than skirmishers.
Heavy Scythed Chariots up to 3	The army can include up to 3 heavy scythed chariots.
Divisions 4+ units	Divisions must contain at least 4 units excluding skirmishers and must be led by a commander.
Skirmishers per division 50% of infantry	Divisions may contain up to half as many skirmisher units as they contain non-skirmisher infantry.

Mithridatic Pontic Troop Values

Unit	Clash	Sustained	Short Range	Long Range	Morale Save	Stamina	Special	Points Value
Pontic heavy cavalry armed with spears and/or javelins	9	6	3	0	4+	6		30 per unit
• Upgrade Pontic heavy cavalry to guard – up to 1 unit	9	6	3	0	4+	6	Valiant	+3 per unit
Sarmatian heavy cavalry with kontos and bows	9	6	3	1	4+	6		34 per unit
• Upgrade Sarmatian cavalry to cataphracts	9	6	3	1	4+	6		+1 per unit
Armenian cataphract cavalry armed with kontos	9	6	3/0	0	4+	6		34 per unit
Scythian horse archers fielded as small units	4	2	2	2	6+	4	Parthian shot	19 per unit
Light cavalry armed with javelins fielded as small units	5	3	2	0	6+	4	Feigned flight	19 per unit
Imitation Roman legionary heavy infantry armed with spears and/or javelins	6	6	3	0	4+	6		24 per unit
Phalangite heavy infantry armed with pikes	7	7	3/0	0	4+	6	Phalanx	32 per unit
• Reduction to field phalangites as former slaves	6	5	1/0	0	6+	6	Phalanx, Levy, Militia	–13 per unit
Galatian medium infantry warband with swords and javelins – up to 1 unit	9	6	2	0	5+	6	Wild fighters	28 per unit
• Extra to field Galatian warband as Bastarnae	9	6	2	0	5+	6	Wild fighters, Fanatic, Frenzied charge	+4 per unit
Subject medium infantry archers	5	5	3	3	5+	6	Levy	21 per unit
• Extra to field subject archers as non-levy – up to half	5	5	3	3	5+	6		+3 per unit
Light infantry mercenary peltasts with spears and/or javelins	5	5	3	0	6+	6		20 per unit
• Extra to field peltasts as Thracians with double-handed rhomphaia – up to 1 unit	6	5	2/0	0	6+	6	Tough fighters	+2 per unit
Thorakitai medium infantry with spears and javelins	6	6	3	0	5+	6		23 per unit
Light infantry archers	4	4	3	3	0	6		20 per unit
• Reduction to field archers as small units	3	3	2	2	0	4		–6 per unit
Skirmishers with javelins fielded as small units	3	2	2	0	0	4		11 per unit
Skirmishers with bows or slings fielded as small units	2	2	2	2	0	4		12 per unit
Heavy scythed chariots fielded as units of 1 model	7	0	0	0	3+	4	Scythed chariot	10 per unit
Commanders			1 commander must be provided per division					Free
			All commanders including general have leadership 8					

The Dacians were barbarians who lived in what is today Romania. They appear to have been close kin of the Thracians with whom they shared a fascination for heavy scythe-like weaponry – known to the Romans as the falx (ie, scythe). Not content with minding their own business, the Dacians raided into Roman territory and were subject to Roman reprisals and eventually conquest by the Emperor Trajan. The Dacians were allied with the Sarmatians who provided heavy bow-armed cavalry. During the Dacians' war against the Romans in the 1st century AD, the Dacian king Decebalus led an army that ambushed and wiped out a Roman legion. The Dacians captured the legion's eagle standard and carried away its artillery which they then used against their former owners with great effect.

Search: Burebista, Domitian's Dacian War, Trajan's Dacian War, Decebalus, Sarmizegetusa, The First Battle of Tapae (87 AD), the Second Battle of Tapae (101 AD).

Infantry 75%+	At least three quarters of the units in the army must be infantry other than skirmishers.
Warbands 50%+ of infantry	At least half the non-skirmisher infantry units in the army must be medium infantry warbands.
Artillery up to 1 unit	The army can have up to one unit of artillery.
Divisions 4+ units	Divisions must contain at least 4 units excluding skirmishers and must be led by a commander.
Skirmishers per division 50% of infantry	Divisions may contain up to half as many skirmisher units as they contain non-skirmisher infantry.

Dacian Troop Values

Unit	Combat				Morale Save	Stamina	Special	Points Value
	Clash	Sustained	Short Range	Long Range				
Medium infantry warbands armed with swords and javelins	9	6	2	0	5+	6		25 per unit
• *Extra to field warbands as falxmen with double-handed weapons – up to half*	10	6	1/0	0	5+	6	*Tough fighters*	+2 per unit
Light infantry archers	4	4	3	3	0	6		20 per unit
• *Reduction to field archers as small units*	3	3	2	2	0	4		–6 per unit
Skirmishers with javelins fielded as small units	3	2	2	0	0	4		11 per unit
Light cavalry armed with javelins and fielded as small units	5	3	2	0	6+	4		17 per unit
Sarmatian light cavalry armed with bows and fielded as small units	5	3	2	2	6+	4		19 per unit
Sarmatian heavy cavalry armed with kontos and bows	9	6	3	1	4+	6		34 per unit
• *Extra to field Sarmatian cavalry as cataphracts*	9	6	3	1	4+	6		+1 per unit
Light artillery bolt throwers	1	1	2	2	0	3		15 per unit
Medium artillery onagers	1	1	0	3	0	3		20 per unit
Commanders	1 commander must be provided per division All commanders including general have leadership 8							Free

MARIAN ROMAN

Armies of the late republic are often described as 'Marian' following the reforms of Gaius Marius in 107 BC. These changes to the rules governing recruitment of the legions standardised equipment and opened the ranks to all classes of citizen. Equipment was now provided by the state rather than by the soldiers themselves. This enabled the Romans to field much larger armies and created a new class of professional soldier. To improve mobility Marius famously did away with much of the baggage train and had the soldiers carry their own equipment – hence the legionaries became known as 'Marius' Mules' ie, carrying their own arms and supplies like mules! This list covers the armies of the brutal Civil Wars that engulfed the Roman world between Sulla's defeat of Marius and Octavian's victory over Mark Antony. As the list includes troops recruited from all over the Roman empire it is necessarily quite long and varied. Like all Roman armies its core remains the heavily armed legionaries. The list also covers the period of Caesar's famous conquest of Gaul and invasion of Britain, as well as Pompey's wars against Pontus, and Crassus' disastrous foray into Parthia.

I have speculatively included the carroballista into the list as these are recorded in later Roman armies. For appropriate rules see the Imperial Roman list. I have made allowance for legionaries fighting in a looser fashion as described for Spanish legions under Sertorius and Pompey. These are treated as light infantry but rated as stubborn to reflect a relatively high level of equipment and discipline. Spanish legions could easily be represented as either medium infantry or regular heavy infantry. I have included the option to illustrate how such things can be arranged for those so inclined.

Search: Marius, Sulla, The Cimbrian War, The Social War, Julius Caesar, The Conquest of Gaul, The Mithridatic Wars, The Roman Civil Wars.

Infantry 50%+	At least half the units in the army must be infantry other than skirmishers.
Cavalry up to 25%	No more than a quarter of the units in the army can be cavalry.
Legions 50%+ of infantry	At least half the non-skirmisher infantry units in the army must be legionaries of one type or another.
Elephant up to 1	The army can include 1 elephant
Artillery	There must be at least three legionary units for every artillery unit fielded, and no more heavy or medium artillery than light artillery units in total.
Divisions 4+ units	Divisions must contain at least 4 units excluding skirmishers and must be led by a commander.
Skirmishers per division 50% of infantry	Divisions may contain up to half as many skirmisher units as they contain non-skirmisher infantry.

Marian Roman Troop Values

Unit	Clash	Sustained	Short Range	Long Range	Morale Save	Stamina	Special	Points Value
Legionary heavy infantry armed with pila and swords	7	7	3	0	4+	6	Drilled, Testudo	32 per unit
• *Extra to upgrade legionaries to veteran – up to half*	7	7	3	0	4+	6	*Drilled, Elite, Testudo*	*+3 per unit*
• *Reduction to downgrade legionaries to raw recruits or imitation legionaries – up to half*	6	6	3	0	4+	6		*–5 per unit*
○ *Reduction to downgrade raw recruits to medium infantry levies*	6	6	3	0	5+	6	*Levy*	*–4 per unit*
Spanish-style light infantry legionaries armed with pila and swords	7	7	3	0	6+	6	Drilled, Testudo, Stubborn	31 per unit
Thracian or Illyrian light infantry armed with javelins and shields – up to 3 units	5	5	3	0	6+	6		20 per unit
• *Extra to field Thracians or Illyrians as mixed javelins and long spears*	5	5	3	0	6+	6		*+3 per unit*
• *Extra to give Thracians double-handed rhomphaia*	6	5	2/0	0	6+	6	*Tough fighters*	*+2 per unit*
Spanish scutarii medium infantry armed with spears	6 6	6 6	3 3	0 0	5+ 5+	6 6		23 per unit 23 per unit
• *Extra to give scutarii heavy javelins counting as pila*	6	6	3	0	5+	6		*+3 per unit*
Gallic or Galatian medium infantry warband armed with swords and javelins – up to 1 unit	9	6	2	0	5+	6	Wild fighters	28 per unit

74

Unit	Combat				Morale Save	Stamina	Special	Points Value
	Clash	Sustained	Short Range	Long Range				
Spanish caetrati light infantry with javelins fielded as small units	3	3	2	0	0	4		12 per unit
Infantry skirmishers armed with javelins and fielded as small units	3	2	2	0	0	4		11 per unit
Skirmishers armed with slings fielded as small units – up to 3 units	2	2	2	2	0	4		12 per unit
• Extra to field sling-armed skirmishers as Balearic slingers – up to 1 unit	2	2	2	2	0	4	Marksmen	+1 point
Skirmishers armed with bows fielded as small units – up to 3 units	2	2	2	2	0	4		12 per unit
• Extra to field bow-armed skirmishers as Cretans – up to 1 unit	2	2	2	2	0	4	Marksmen	+1 per unit
German medium cavalry armed with spears and/or javelins	8	5	3	0	5+	6	Tough fighters, Stubborn	30 per unit
Gallic medium cavalry armed with spears and/or javelins	8	5	3	0	5+	6	Tough fighters	28 per unit
Spanish medium cavalry armed with spears and/or javelins	8	5	3	0	5+	6		27 per unit
Caetrati light infantry with javelins fielded as small sub-units of Spanish cavalry – 1 per Spanish medium cavalry unit	3	3	2	0	0	4	Sub-unit of Spanish cavalry	12 per unit
Spanish, Thracian or Cappadocian light cavalry armed with javelins and fielded as small units	5	3	2	0	6+	4		17 per unit
Numidian light cavalry with javelins fielded as small units	5	3	2	0	6+	4	Feigned flight	19 per unit
Syrian light cavalry with bows fielded as a small unit – up to 1 unit	5	3	2	2	6+	4	Feigned flight	21 per unit
Arab camel-mounted light cavalry with bows and javelins fielded as a small unit – up to 1 unit	4	3	2	2	6+	4	Feigned flight	20 per unit
Light artillery scorpion bolt throwers	1	1	2	2	0	3	Drilled	18 per unit
• Extra to mount scorpion on carts as carroballista	1	1	2	2	0	3	Drilled	+3 per unit
Medium artillery onagers	1	1	0	3	0	3		20 per unit
Heavy artillery ballistae	1	1	0	3	0	3		23 per unit
Elephant with javelin-armed crew	4	3	1	0	4+	6	Elephant	23 per unit
Commanders	1 commander must be provided per division All commanders including general have leadership 8							Free
• Extra to upgrade general to leadership 9	The general can have leadership 9 at the following extra cost							+25

THE PERSIANS ACCORDING TO MAURICE

'The Persian nation is wicked, dissembling, and servile, but at the same time patriotic and obedient,' is the Byzantine Emperor Maurice's somewhat damning overview of his eastern neighbours in the Strategikon. He goes on to describe how their armies are particularly skilled at siegecraft, and he gives an account of their weapons and tactics. He says, 'In fighting against lancers they hasten to form their battle line in the roughest terrain, and to use their bows, so that the charge of the lancers against them will be dissipated and broken up by the rough ground.' He also describes them as 'marching step-by-step in even and dense formation' and explains how they attack at the hottest hour of the day once the heat has weakened their enemy's spirits. He makes it clear that the Persians' strength lay in their archery and stresses how important it was to close quickly, 'for any delay in closing with the enemy means that their steady rate of fire will enable them to discharge more missiles against our soldiers and horses.'

Early stone Egyptian mace head
Early dynastic period c. 2900-2500 BC
(Perry Collection)

The basic legionary is a formidable warrior, and I have allowed both upgrades and downgrades to represent the varying quality of different legions over time. Further subtleties of differentiation could easily be applied where the record merits them. In the case of auxiliary infantry cohorts I have given a full range of stats as light, medium and heavy infantry and leave the player to suit the type to his own army. As a general principle it is assumed that auxiliaries begin the period as light troops and evolve into more typical battle line formations over time. The usual Roman 'heavy' cavalry are represented as 'medium cavalry' as this is my standard interpretation for most heavily armed cavalry of the classical era – this is not a mistake – but players who take umbrage with my judgement are perfectly welcome to adjust things to their satisfaction. Having said that, I have allowed for the one known unit of 'cataphracts' ala I Gallorum et Pannoniorum (stationed in Moesia), though I have slightly toned down the fighting stats of these compared to dedicated horse-riding armies. Camel-mounted troops were known only in the East. Eastern legionaries were notoriously soft, so at least 1 unit of Legionaries must be fielded as raw recruits if camels are included. Carroballistae are scorpions mounted onto mule carts. They move at infantry rate and can make up to three moves and shoot in the same turn. They cannot traverse terrain unsuitable for wheeled vehicles, but the carts can be abandoned at any time and the scorpions deployed on foot.

Note that marines are accounted for within the entry for medium infantry auxiliaries whilst Praetorians can be rated as legionaries or veterans as required. I can see no justification for auxiliaries carrying other than generalised spears and javelins and so have not allowed for it. I have also allowed for Roman legionaries equipped with extra armour as 'Dacian-fighters' by the simple expedient of making them stubborn. Player who wish to interpret these things differently are, of course, entirely welcome to do so.

Search: The Roman Conquest of Britain, The Parthian War, The Jewish Revolt, The Civil War of 69 AD, The Dacian Wars, the Marcomannic Wars.

Infantry 50%+	At least half the units in the army must be infantry other than skirmishers.
Legions 25%+ of infantry	At least a quarter of the non-skirmisher infantry units in the army must be legionaries of one type or another.
Cavalry up to 25%	Up to a quarter of the units in the army can be cavalry.
Artillery	There must be at least three legionary units for every artillery unit fielded, and no more heavy or medium artillery than light artillery units in total.
Divisions 4+ units	Divisions must contain at least 4 units excluding skirmishers and must be led by a commander.
Skirmishers per division 50% of infantry	Divisions can contain up to half as many skirmisher units as they contain non-skirmisher infantry.

Imperial Roman Troop Values

Unit	Combat				Morale Save	Stamina	Special	Points Value
	Clash	Sustained	Short Range	Long Range				
Legionary heavy infantry armed with pila and swords	7	7	3	0	4+	6	Drilled, Testudo	32 per unit
• Extra to upgrade legionaries to elite – up to half	7	7	3	0	4+	6	Drilled, Elite, Testudo	+3 per unit
• Extra to make any of the above stubborn as Dacian-fighters - up to half	7	7	3	0	4+	6	As above +Stubborn	+3 per unit
Veteran legionary heavy infantry armed with pila and swords – up to 1 unit	7	7	3	0	4+	6	Drilled, Elite, Testudo Tough fighters, Stubborn	39 per unit
Legionary raw recruit heavy infantry armed with pila and swords	6	6	3	0	4+	6		27 per unit
Auxiliary medium infantry with spears	6	6	3	0	5+	6		23 per unit
• Extra to upgrade auxiliary medium infantry to heavy infantry	7	7	3	0	4+	6		+3 per unit
• Extra to upgrade auxiliary medium or heavy infantry to elite – up to half			As above				Elite	+3 per unit
• Extra to upgrade auxiliary medium or heavy infantry to veterans – up to 1 unit			As above				Elite, Tough fighters	+4 per unit
Auxiliary light infantry with spears and/or javelins	5	5	3	0	6+	6		20 per unit

Unit	Combat				Morale Save	Stamina	Special	Points Value
	Clash	Sustained	Short Range	Long Range				
Auxiliary medium infantry archers	5	5	3	3	5+	6		24 per unit
Auxiliary light infantry archers	4	4	3	3	6+	6		21 per unit
• *Reduction to field archers as small units*	3	3	2	2	6+	4		–6 per unit
Skirmishers armed with javelins and fielded as small units	3	2	2	0	0	4		11 per unit
Skirmishers armed with slings or bows and fielded as small units	2	2	2	2	0	4		12 per unit
Auxiliary medium cavalry with spears and/or javelins	8	5	3	0	5+	6		27 per unit
• *Extra to give medium cavalry kontos – up to 1 unit*	8	5	3/0	0	5+	6		+3 per unit
Auxiliary heavy cavalry with spears and/or javelins – up to 1 unit	8	5	3	0	4+	6		28 per unit
• *Extra to make auxiliary heavy cavalry cataphracts*	8	5	3	0	4+	6		+1 per unit
Auxiliary light cavalry armed with javelins and fielded as small units	5	3	2	0	6+	4		17 per unit
• *Extra to upgrade auxiliary light cavalry to Numidians – up to 1 unit*	5	3	2	0	6+	4	*Feigned flight*	+2 per unit
Auxiliary light cavalry armed with bows and fielded as small units	5	3	2	2	6+	4	Feigned flight	21 per unit
Camel-mounted light cavalry with bows and javelins fielded as a small unit – up to 1 unit	4	3	2	2	6+	4	Feigned flight	20 per unit
Light artillery scorpion bolt throwers	1	1	2	2	0	3	Drilled	18 per unit
• *Extra to mount scorpions on carts as carroballistae*	1	1	2	2	0	3	*Drilled*	+3 per unit
Medium artillery onagers	1	1	0	3	0	3		20 per unit
Heavy artillery ballistae	1	1	0	3	0	3		23 per unit
Commanders	1 commander must be provided per division All commanders including general have leadership 8							Free
• *Extra to upgrade general to leadership 9*	*The general can have leadership 9 at the following extra cost*							+25

Form testudo!

This list represents the army of the People's Popular Front for Judea and can, with suitable modification, be used to represent the very similar forces of the Judean People's Popular Front (splitters!). In fact it represents the troops commanded and described by Josephus, who rose against the Romans and were eventually defeated by Vespasian and his son Titus. The list can also be pressed into service to describe the armies of the numerous Jewish revolts, which seem to have been a feature of life in ancient Judea. The terms zealots and sicarii are not strictly accurate for the whole period covered, but I've used them as descriptions for various religiously motivated and fanatical fighters. The provision of a few cavalry is attested from the first Jewish War, but seems a reasonable assumption for all of these revolts.

Search: Zealots, Titus and the Siege of Jerusalem, Battle of Beth Horon 66 AD, The Great Revolt, Masada, The Kitos War, The Bar Kokhba Revolt.

Cavalry up to 10%	Up to one in ten of the units in the army can be cavalry.
Infantry 75%+	At least three quarters of the units in the army must be infantry other than skirmishers.
Light Infantry javelins 50%+ of infantry	At least half the non-skirmish infantry in the army must be light infantry units armed with javelins, improvised weapons and daggers or similarly armed zealots, sicarii or levy.
Divisions 4+ units.	Divisions must contain at least 4 units excluding skirmishers and must be led by a commander.
Skirmishers per division 100% of infantry/cavalry	Divisions may contain up to as many skirmisher units as they contain non-skirmisher infantry and/or cavalry units.

Jewish Revolt Troop Values

Unit	Clash	Sustained	Short Range	Long Range	Morale Save	Stamina	Special	Points Value
Light infantry with javelins, improvised weapons, and daggers	5	5	3	0	6+	6		20 per unit
• *Reduction to make light infantry levy*	5	5	3	0	6+	6	Levy	−3 per unit
• *Extra to make light infantry zealots*	6	5	3	0	6+	6	Wild fighters	+4 per unit
○ *Extra to make zealots sicarii – up to half*	6	5	3	0	6+	6	Wild fighters, Fanatics, Valiant	+4 per unit
Light infantry with bows	4	4	3	3	0	6		20 per unit
• *Extra to make light infantry bowmen zealots*	4	4	3	3	6+	6	Fanatics	+2 per unit
• *Reduction to make non-zealot bowmen levy*	4	4	3	3	0	6	Levy	−3 per unit
Skirmishers with javelins fielded as small units	3	2	2	0	0	4		11 per unit
Skirmishers with slings fielded as small units	2	2	2	2	0	4		12 per unit
Skirmishers with bows fielded as small units	2	2	2	2	0	4		12 per unit
Light cavalry armed with javelins and fielded as small units	5	3	2	0	6+	4		17 per unit
Commanders		1 commander must be provided per division. All commanders including general have leadership 8.						Free

The Kushan (nothing to do with soft furnishings) were a Scythian tribe who established themselves in the old Bactrian Greek and Indo-Greek kingdoms and went on to occupy much of northern India and eastern Parthia (the Indo-Parthian Kingdom based at Taxila). The army is a fascinating mix of Scythian style cavalry and Indian infantry, but could also include some of the Bactrian Greek elements in the early part of the period covered – see the Bactrian Greek list for suitable stats.

Search: Yuezhi, Indo-Scythians, Saka, Kujula Kadphises, Kanishka, Gandhara.

Cavalry 50%+	At least half of the units in the army must be cavalry.
Horse archers 50%+ of cavalry	At least half of the cavalry units in the army must be horse archers
Infantry 25%+	At least a quarter of the units in the army must be infantry other than skirmishers.
Elephants up to 10%	Up to one in ten of the units in the army can be elephants.
Divisions 4+ units	Divisions must contain at least 4 units excluding skirmishers and must be led by a commander.
Skirmishers per division 50% of infantry	Divisions may contain up to half as many skirmisher units as they contain non-skirmisher infantry.

Kushan Troop Values

Unit	Clash	Sustained	Short Range	Long Range	Morale Save	Stamina	Special	Points Value
Kushan heavy cavalry armed with kontos	9	6	3/0	0	4+	6		33 per unit
Kushan horse archers fielded as small units	4	2	2	2	6+	4	Parthian shot	19 per unit
Light cavalry armed with spears and/or javelins and bows fielded as small units	5	3	2	2	6+	4	Feigned flight	21 per unit
Indian medium cavalry with spears and/or javelins	8	5	3	0	5+	6		27 per unit
Indian light cavalry with spears and/or javelins	7	5	3	0	6+	6		25 per unit
Indian or Kushan light cavalry armed with spears and/or javelins and bows fielded as small units	5	3	2	2	6+	4	Feigned flight	21 per unit
Indian medium infantry armed with spears and/or javelins	6	6	3	0	5+	6		23 per unit
Indian medium infantry archers	5	5	3	3	5+	6		24 per unit
Indian, Kushan or Parthian light infantry archers	4	4	3	3	0	6		20 per unit
• Reduction to field archers as small units	3	3	2	2	0	4		–6 per unit
Skirmishers with javelins fielded as small units	3	2	2	0	0	4		11 per unit
Skirmishers with bows fielded as small unit	2	2	2	2	0	4		12 per unit
Elephants with crew armed with spears, javelins and bows	4	3	1	1	4+	6	Elephant	24 per unit
Skirmishers armed with javelins fielded as a as small unit – up to 1 per elephant	3	2	2	0	0	4	Sub-unit of elephant	11 per unit
Commanders			1 commander must be provided per division All commanders including general have leadership 8					Free

> "The war of the Jews against the Romans was the greatest of our time; greater too, perhaps than any recorded struggle between cities or nations."

Josephus, *The Jewish War*

APPENDIX

POINTS VALUES

The points values given throughout this book are based on a simple formula: adding up all the stats to get a base value. For example, here is the stat-line for Persian sparabara medium infantry.

Unit	Combat				Morale Save	Stamina	Special	Points Value
	Clash	Sustained	Short Range	Long Range				
Iranian/Mede sparabara medium infantry with mixed spears and bows	6	6	3	3	5+	6	Sparabara	26 per unit

The value is 6+6+3+3+(2)+6 = 26 points. The value of the Morale Save (2) is the number of successful roll combinations on a single dice, so a save of 6 = 1 (1 in 6 chance), a save of 5+ = 2 (2 in 6 chance), a save of 4+ = 3 (3 in 6 chance) and a save of 3+ = 4 (4 in 6 chance). The sparabara special rule is free as noted on page 31.

Although the real worth of the different game stats are not necessarily exactly equal, this simple formula works well enough because all the stats of the different types are closely linked. Thus units with good Morale also have high fighting values, whilst small units with low Stamina also have lowered fighting values. Stamina is also fixed fairly rigidly within the lists, so although it is arguably worth the most per increment, its value is the same for all standard sized units.

TROOP TYPES

The stat lines take no account of movement rates, or of the rules applying to the different types of units. The following modifiers are therefore applied throughout the lists.

Type of unit	Points added to cost		
	Standard	Small	Large
Cavalry and chariots	+3	+2	+4
Cataphract cavalry	+1 (ie. +4 in total)	+1	+1
Scythed chariot	10 pts total	N/A	N/A
Light artillery	+6	+4	+8
Medium artillery	+12	+8	+16
Heavy artillery	+15	+10	+20
Elephant	+6	N/A	N/A
Cart-mounted infantry or artillery	+3	+2	+4

Note that very few large units are included in the lists and where given they are optional. Nonetheless, I have included the theoretical modifiers in the chart above for anyone wanting to make use of them.

The extra point for cataphracts may not seem much, but the loss of mobility compared to heavy cavalry is a big reduction in their effectiveness and is felt to balance out. The values for artillery reflect their extra range and the relative unimportance of the rest of their stat line.

I realise that there are some inherent abilities of different troop types that are not taken into account in the points values – they are freebies. For example, the ability of heavy infantry to close ranks, and the 'to hit' modifier that applies when shooting at them. Similarly, the ability of light infantry to fight in loose order, and for loose order troops to evade, is not costed separately. These things are judged to be either part-and-parcel of a unit's role or else too minor to be worth consideration.

WEAPONS

The following modifiers are applied to units carrying weapons that have their own 'useful' rules. Note that weapons are indicated under the unit column, they are not included under the special rules column. No specific rules or points modifiers apply to other weapons.

Weapons carried	Points added to cost		
	Standard	Small	Large
Kontos	3	2	4
Lance	3	2	4
Long spear	3	2	4
Pike	3	2	4
Pilum/equivalent	3	2	4
Double-handed weapon	1	1	1
Crossbow	Free	Free	Free
Sling	Free	Free	Free

Where troops are armed with a mix of spears or javelins I usually use the phrase 'spears and/or javelins' and this is intended to cover all kinds of spears of various lengths, whether thrown or thrust, where no special rules apply and armament is represented wholly by the stats. No cost is applied to units carrying these weapons or to those armed with swords or similar arms that are represented entirely by means of the stat line.

The term 'long spear' is specifically used to describe troops with long spears fighting in a particular, regular, dense style. It is associated with a useful rule and a split short range stat. Bear in mind that troops fighting in a looser style, or lacking proper training or formation, could conceivably carry spears that are long, but which don't qualify for the 'long spear' rule and which are therefore just described as 'spear' or 'spear and/or javelin in the lists'.

Note that the reason double-handed weapons have a lower points cost than other hand-to-hand combat weapons is that much of their value is reflected in the (neutral overall) stat adjustment. Pike always have the additional points added for 'phalanx' (see below). Long spears sometimes have the 'phalanx' rule, but not always. Crossbows and slings have benefits and also disadvantages compared to bows, and are therefore cost neutral.

SPECIAL RULES

The special rules column indicates which useful rules, if any, have been applied to that entry, apart from useful rules for weapons, which are included in the unit type description.

Rule	Summary of Rule	Points added to cost		
		Standard	Small	Large
Brave	Shaken units rally on D6 roll of 4+ at end of command phase if more than 12" from enemy	3	2	4
Drilled	Free move on failed order. Units may move through other drilled units without risk of disorder	3	2	4
Eager	Free move on charge order given within maximum charge distance	Free	Free	Free
Elite	Recover from disorder on D6 roll of 4+ at start of turn	3	2	4
Fanatic	Morale Save +1 until shaken	1	1	1
Feigned flight	The unit is allowed to move out of a combat engagement	3	2	4
Frenzied charge	Must charge if within range, with 3 moves allowed on any successful order/initiative	3	2	4
Freshly raised	Check unit in first round of combat as per the Hail Caesar rulebook	-1	-1	-1
Levy	Must roll 4+ on a D6 to recover disorder at end of turn	-3	-2	-4
Marauders	Ignore distance penalty for command	3	2	4
Marksmen	Re-roll one missed ranged attack	1	1	1
Militia	No move on roll equal to commander's leadership when given orders	-3	-2	-4
Parthian shot	Can evade and make closing shots as a reaction to an enemy charge	3	2	4
Phalanx	Lost combats up to 2 count as draws until the unit is shaken	3	2	4
Pig's head formation	Fighting unit can be supported by 2 friends to the rear	Free	Free	Free

Rule	Summary of Rule	Points added to cost		
		Standard	Small	Large
Steady	Ignore the first '6' rolled for break tests from ranged attacks each turn	3	2	4
Stubborn	Re-roll 1 failed morale save if save is 6	1	1	1
	Re-roll 1 failed morale save if save is 5+	2	2	2
	Re-roll 1 failed morale save if save is 4+	3	3	3
	Re-roll 1 failed morale save if save is 3+	4	4	4
Sub-unit	Unit and sub-unit must remain within 1 move	Free	Free	Free
Testudo formation	Free move	Free	Free	Free
	+2 morale saves from ranged attacks			
	Counts 'front' all round to missiles			
	Make no ranged attacks			
	Adopt battle line if engaged			
Tough fighters	Re-roll one missed hand-to-hand combat attack	1	1	1
Valiant	Break test re-roll once per battle	3	2	4
Wavering	Take a break test each time you take a casualty	Half total	Half total	Half total
Wedge formation	Free move	Free (but not suitable for matched games)		
	Counts 'front' all round to missiles			
	Counts 'front' all round for own ranged attacks			
	+1 morale save against all attacks			
	Cannot support or be supported except by enclosed friends			
	Can make own attacks all round			
	Enemy giving ground to front are burst through			
	Wedge can make three moves through enemy it has burst through			
Wild fighters	Re-roll up to 3 missed hand-to-hand combat attacks in their first round of combat	3	3	3

On the whole the bonus for most special rules is fixed at 3 points in the case of a standard-sized unit as you can see from the chart above. Admittedly, this is not a precise reflection of value in all cases, but it is good enough to serve our purposes and to differentiate between the common and enhanced units.

Where a special rule is equivalent to an extra increment of a stat, the value is considered to be the same as if this were a stat increase – ie, 1 point per increment. The same applies to re-rolls, for example tough fighters and stubborn. Wild fighters is costed at the full 3 points even though it is only used once; this is on the basis that it is up to the player to make use of the ability when it counts!

Some abilities are free. Eager, for example, is considered as much of a liability as an advantage and is therefore offered at no cost. Formation based abilities are also free, including sub-units. This is because it is rather difficult to fix a value on abilities that are likely to see little use on an open field, or which offer no significant advantage as in the case of the sub-unit and pig's head. The wedge formation is considered suitable only for scenarios and is best avoided in matched games; no units have been given this ability in the lists.

The adjustment for wavering units is to halve the unit's total points value. This is felt to be a fair reflection of the considerable risk of fielding them.

A Greek phalanx prepares to advance.

COMMON USEFUL RULES

When it came to creating broadly based lists we decided against using some of the rules, these being judged suitable only in very specific circumstances – for example the wedge formation as noted above. A few are only used occasionally to reflect unusual troop types. Others find common employment because they reflect general advantages or universal characteristics. This section explains why certain rules are commonly applied, and will hopefully prove useful to anyone contemplating creating their own lists or tinkering with those provided.

Drilled. We kept this one for regular drilled troops such as Romans, Hellenistic armies and Byzantines. Although it might be arguably extended to many more armies, our choice was to retain it as a distinguishing feature of these and comparable regular armies.

Eager. Eager is usually applied to barbarian troops known for being keen to get to close-quarters. The troops are difficult to restrain in the face of the enemy.

Elite. The elite rule is always applied as Elite 4+ in the lists. This means the unit will recover from disorder on the roll of a 4, 5 or 6 made at the start of the turn. We apply this rule to very highly trained and motivated regular troops and often to regular guards or the equivalent. It is not usually applied to barbarian armies or armies generally lacking in training or experience. Often it is applied only to a single unit in the army.

Feigned flight. This rule is usually applied to small units of light cavalry equipped primarily for skirmishing. It is not normally applied to standard sized units.

Levy. The levy rule is preferred to represent poorly trained, inexperienced, or unenthusiastic troops. The alternative militia rule tends to slow the game down and presents an obstacle to the player moving his army; this works better in larger games and scenarios where these things can be compensated for.

Marksmen. The marksmen ability is often given to specialist units of infantry skirmishers such as Cretan archers, Balearic slings, and so on.

Parthian shot. This rule is usually applied to skilled horse archers, including all nomad types as well as Parthians.

Stubborn. The stubborn rule is sometimes given to highly motivated troops to reflect their willingness to die fighting. It is also sometimes used to represent troops that are especially heavily armoured for their type, e.g. front rank Byzantine kontaratoi.

Tough fighters. This ability is often given to barbarian guard or the personal retainers of a chieftain – it is the barbarian equivalent to the elite rule. It can also be given to other troops, whether regular or barbarian, to represent veterans or just 'tough fighters'.

Wild fighters. Wild fighters is always applied with three re-rolls in the lists and a cost of +3 points. This is the standard ability for early barbarian warbands such as Gauls, Britons, and Germans.

INFANTRY OF THE BIBLICAL & CLASSICAL ERAS

Broadly speaking, I treat all biblical era close fighting infantry as medium as this establishes a relationship between the infantry and chariots that feels about right. Because of this bowmen are relatively powerful in these armies – as was often the case historically – and the exchange of missiles becomes an important part of the battle.

Heavy infantry become a feature of classical armies, and with their ability to close ranks and withstand missile fire they rise to prominence as the real battle winners. This downgrades archery to a supporting role in most armies. On the whole cavalry are still relatively weak, a reflection on the size and breeding of horses, lack of stirrups, developed saddles and horseshoes. I therefore count battle line cavalry as medium in most cases rather than heavy, and this establishes the relationship between infantry and cavalry. Of course, there are some horse-riding cultures where the cavalry represent a heavily armed and armoured elite as represented by heavy cavalry and cataphracts – such as the Sarmatians and Parthians, and later the Sassanid Persians. It is significant that these are the very armies that gave Roman infantry such trouble!

Effective battle line cavalry become a feature of the armies of late antiquity and afterwards, as we shall describe in the next volume of army lists for Hail Caesar.

Take that, Marcus! A splendid conversion using Warlord Games plastic Celt and Imperial Roman legionary miniatures.

Put your back into it, you 'orrible little men! Imperial Roman legionaries prepare a marching fort.

Forward sons of Sparta! Hoplite phalanx arrayed for battle.

For the glory of Rome! Imperial Roman auxiliaries charge upon their foes.